RETURNING
EXERCISES IN REPENTANCE

Edited by

JONATHAN MAGONET

BLOCH PUBLISHING COMPANY, INC.
New York, N.Y.

First published in 1975
by The Reform Synagogues of Great Britain
33 Seymour Place London W1H 5AP
© 1975 The Reform Synagogues of Great Britain
First United States Printing 1978
by Bloch Publishing Company, Inc.
Library of Congress Catalog Number: 78-68143
I.S.B.N. 0-8197-0468-7

All rights reserved, including the right to reproduce
this book or portions thereof in any form.

PREFACE

"Turn us back to You Lord,
and we shall return;
renew our lives as of old."

הֲשִׁיבֵנוּ יְיָ אֵלֶיךָ וְנָשׁוּבָה
חַדֵּשׁ יָמֵינוּ כְּקֶדֶם

INTRODUCTION

The language of prayer is difficult in our time. It is a secular age, in which man and his achievements take the centre of the stage, and he is the measure by which everything must be judged. But prayer tells us that there is another centre, both within and beyond us, and that it is we who are measured and judged. To shift our attention to God requires an effort of imagination, humility and will. In our tradition it is called *"Teshuvah"* — "turning", "return".

This anthology has been prepared in conjunction with a revision of the High Holyday liturgy. It is hoped that the material gathered here will help on their way anyone who would take the path of *"Teshuvah"*.

The passages have been chosen because they say something — sometimes at once, sometimes after further study, for religion is not just slogans, but speaks to the complexities of life. They can be used for private meditation, for group or Synagogue study, within the service or outside it.

All the contributors are Jews — though a generous interpretation has been given to this word. They come from all periods, sections and traditions, and from no tradition — because the word of God is heard not only in temples, but also in places that seem a wilderness, and not all who hear it are saints. The private experience, the minority view, these have always been expressed in the Bible and Talmud alongside the "normative", and we are so poor in teachers today that we can afford to neglect no-one.

In the recent past we have seen the dimensions of sin and suffering on one hand, goodness, virtue and wisdom on the other — they are realities, and we know that there is a difference between them as between darkness and light. The High Holydays speak about this difference, if we can only begin to grasp their meaning. They make us conscious of the work of purification that has to be done — and that the most important, and natural, place to start, is with ourselves.

JONATHAN MAGONET

CONTENTS

	Page
RESPONSIBILITY – *For oneself*	1
– *For Israel*	2
– *Seeking the Hand of God*	4
TRUTH	8
PURIFICATION	12
SIN – *Categories*	13
– *Free Will*	13
– *The Two Impulses*	14
– *Controlling the Impulse to Evil*	16
– *Its Recognition*	17
– *Its Effect*	18
– *Its Antidote*	18
– *In Business*	19
– *Of Pride*	21
– *Of Anger*	22
– *Of Prejudice*	22
– *Of "Slander"*	23
– *Of "Flattery"*	24
– *Of Religion*	25
CHESHBON HANEFESH – *Self Judgment*	29
JUDGMENT	30
JUDGMENT AND MERCY	32
TESHUVAH – *Repentance*	32
– *Conscience*	33
– *Meaning*	34
– *Turning About*	35
– *Its Power*	35
– *Between Man and Man*	37
– *Forgiving Others*	37
– *Man and God*	39

TESHUVAH *(Cont)*

	Page
– *Preparation*	40
– *The Timing*	41
– *Aids*	42
– *Hindrances*	43
– *The Struggle*	45
– *The Boundaries*	46
– *True and False*	47
– *Israel*	47
– *The World*	49
– *and Messiah*	49
– *Baaley Teshuvah (Penitents)*	49
– *Meditations*	51
– *First or Last*	54
TEFILAH – *Prayer*	54
ZEDAKAH – *Charity*	58
ATONEMENT	60
– *Intimations*	61
HIGH HOLYDAYS	61
ROSH HASHANAH – *The Birthday of the World*	63
– *Meditations*	64
SHALIACH TZIBBUR	67
KITTEL	68
FASTING	69
CONFESSION	71
– *The Problem*	73
MALCHUYOT – *Kingship of God*	75
THE SHOFAR	76
TEN DAYS – *Meditations*	79
KOL NIDRE – *Meaning*	82
– *Meditations*	83
DAY OF ATONEMENT – *Meaning*	86
– *Meditations*	86
MARTYROLOGY	89
AVODAH – *The Ritual*	99
– *Sacrifice*	100
– *Kneeling*	102
MEMORIAL PRAYERS – *Meditations*	102
NEILAH	106
BEFORE THE LAW	108
GLOSSARY	110
ACKNOWLEDGMENTS	120

RESPONSIBILITY – *For Oneself*

If I am not for myself, who is for me? But if I am only for myself, what am I? And if not now, when?
HILLEL

Everything is in the hand of God except the fear of God.
BERACHOT

Everything is foreseen, yet free choice is granted. The world is judged with mercy, yet everything is according to the amount of work. Everything is given on pledge, and a net is spread for all living. The shop is open, and the shopkeeper gives credit, and the account is open and the hand writes, and whoever wishes to borrow may come and borrow. But the collectors go round every day, and exact payment from man with his consent or without it, and their claims are justified, and the judgment is a judgment of truth.
Yet everything is prepared for the feast!
AKIBA

There are all sorts of flight from responsibility: There is flight into death, flight into sickness, and finally flight into folly. The last is the least dangerous and most convenient; and even to the wise, the way to it is usually not as far as they like to imagine.
ARTHUR SCHNITZLER

One of the ways in which some prisoners tried to protect their integration was to feel newly important because their suffering protected others. After all, concentration camp prisoners had been singled out for punishment by the SS as representative of all the dissatisfied elements.
This having to suffer for others was used by many prisoners to pacify inner guilt over their antisocial behaviour in the camps, while the actually unbearable living conditions were used to rationalize such behaviour toward others. Indication of this were to be found whenever one prisoner called another one to task for misbehaviour ... the typical response was: "I can't be normal when I have to live in such circumstances".
By a parallel reasoning they felt they had atoned for any shortcomings in the past, whether in themselves or in their relations to family and friends, as well as any future changes they might still undergo. They felt free to deny responsibility or guilt on a number of scores, felt free to hate other people, including their own families, even where the shortcomings were obviously their own ...

RESPONSIBILITY – *For Oneself*

Such defences, aimed at retaining self respect by denying all guilt, actually weakened the prisoners' personalities: by blaming outside forces for their actions, they not only denied having personal control of their lives, but also that what they did was of any consequence. Blaming others, or outside conditions for one's own misbehaviour may be the child's privilege; if an adult denies responsibility for his actions, it is another step toward personality disintegration.
BRUNO BETTELHEIM

RESPONSIBILITY – *For Israel*

If there is one righteous man, the whole world exists for his sake. If one man sins, the whole generation suffers on account of him. This is the law of solidarity in Israel and the world.
A. MARMORSTEIN

All Jews are sureties for one another.
SIFRA

"Israel is a scattered sheep" (*Jeremiah 50:17*). Why are the Israelites compared to a sheep? Just as if you strike a sheep on its head, or on one of its limbs, all its limbs feel it, so, if one Israelite sins, all Israelites feel it. R. Simeon b. Yohai said: It is as if there are men in a boat, and one man takes a drill, and begins to bore a hole beneath him. His companions say "What are you doing? " He replies, "What business is it of yours? Am I not boring under myself? " They answer, "It is our business, because the water will come in, and swamp the boat with us in it".
LEVITICUS RABBAH

All those who are in a position to reprove the members of their household, and do not do so are held accountable for the sins of the members of their household; those who are in a position to reprove the people of their city, and do not do so, are held accountable for the sins of the people of their city; and those who are in a position to reprove all men, and do not do so, are held accountable for the sins of all men.
SHABBAT

One should feel the suffering of his neighbour, so that when he prays he shall pray for his neighbour too ... If he does not commiserate with the suffering of others, how does he expect that God will commiserate with him and answer his prayers?
SEFER CHASIDIM

RESPONSIBILITY — *For Israel*

We Jews have a more pressing responsibility for our lives and beliefs than perhaps any other religious community.
Don't shelter yourself in any course of action by the idea that "it is my affair". It is your affair, but it is also mine and the community's. Nor can we neglect the world beyond. A fierce light beats upon the Jew. It is a grave responsibility this — to be a Jew; and you can't escape from it, even if you choose to ignore it. Ethically or religiously, we Jews can be and do nothing light-heartedly. Ten bad Jews may help to damn us; ten good Jews may help to save us. Which *minyan* will you join?

C. G. MONTEFIORE

At the beginning of the Atonement service the most venerable men in the congregation solemnly repeat from the *Almemor*: "With the permission of the Court on High, and with the permission of the Congregation below, we declare it permitted to pray with hardened transgressors". Why this custom? In some communities of the Middle Ages there were persons who, by their conduct, had placed themselves outside the pale of Judaism; cowardly apostates, for example, who sold their souls; informers, who spread broadcast false accusations against their brethren; insubordinates, outcasts, criminals. Throughout the year those never sought spiritual fellowship with their brethren. On Yom Kippur, however, they would steal into some corner of the synagogue and join the worshippers in prayer. The Rabbis thereupon instituted this solemn declaration, in order to proclaim in most unmistakable terms that, no matter what is a man's mode of life — slanderer, apostate, outcast — he is still a brother. "*We* have transgressed, *we* have dealt treacherously, *we* have robbed", do we pray. We associate ourselves with the most forlorn souls that sin in darkness, because we recognize that society — we ourselves — are largely responsible for their actions. Many a time has our evil example misled others, become a stumbling-block in the way of the blind. And all our Yom Kippur vows to rise to a higher life are useless, unless we endeavour to raise others who have fallen.

J. H. HERTZ

Who is a Jew? The question remains often more important than the answers. It is a question, which makes us face a mystery. Man who encounters a mystery cannot but wonder and marvel. The Jew has something to do with God.
The question "Who is a Jew?" burdens the individual Jew and challenges him. Can the individual Jew answer a question which requires the consideration of the whole of Jewish history? The answer

RESPONSIBILITY – *For Israel*

forces the individual Jew to represent the whole Jewish people. No Jew can run away from his fate, from the conditions of his Jewish existence. The Jew is chosen. He may bless the Lord who has chosen him. He may curse his election, which does not let him go. The Jew is anchored in his Jewish fate. Anyone who asks the question "Who is a Jew?" must be prepared to see an ordinary man, a man like any other man, but involved and implicated in the holy state of being elected by God.
IGNAZ MAYBAUM

RESPONSIBILITY – *Seeking the Hand of God*

What was really needed was a fundamental change in our attitude toward life. We had to learn ourselves and, furthermore, we had to teach the despairing men (in the concentration camp), that it did not really matter what we expected from life, but rather what life expected from us. We needed to stop asking about the meaning of life, and instead to think of ourselves as those who were being questioned by life – daily and hourly. Our answer must consist, not in talk and meditation, but in right action and in right conduct. Life ultimately means taking the responsibility to find the right answer to its problems and to fulfill the tasks which it constantly sets for each individual ...
When a man finds that it is his destiny to suffer, he will have to accept his suffering as his task; his single and unique task. He will have to acknowledge the fact that even in suffering he is unique and alone in the universe. No one can relieve him of his suffering or suffer in his place. His unique opportunity lies in the way in which he bears his burden.
VIKTOR E. FRANKL

Nothing comes to man except by the decree of the Holy One blessed be He. One should pray for God's mercy that whatever is decreed shall turn out for the sake of heaven.
SEFER CHASIDIM

If a man dislike his wife, he should not pray that God give him another wife, but rather, if she annoys him or is displeasing in his eyes, he should pray that God turn her heart to love him and to find favour in his eyes – so that they should renew their love for one another ...
If one has an enemy, he should pray to the Holy One, not to slay or punish his enemy, but rather to help them both bring about peace ... In times of war, the prayer should not be for victory of the one side over the other, but it should be for peace – that the Holy One blessed be He influence their hearts that they make peace.
SEFER CHASIDIM

RESPONSIBILITY – *Seeking the Hand of God*

The environment which I feel to be the natural one, the situation which has been assigned to me as my fate, the things that happen to me day after day, the things that claim me day after day – these contain my essential task and such fulfilment of existence as is open to me ...

The Baal-Shem teaches that no encounter with a being or a thing in the course of our life lacks a hidden significance. The people we live with or meet with, the animals that help us with our farmwork, the soil we till, the materials we shape, the tools we use, they all contain a mysterious spiritual substance which depends on us for helping it towards its pure form, its perfection. If we neglect this spiritual substance sent across our path, if we think only in terms of momentary purposes, without developing a genuine relationship to the beings and things in whose life we ought to take part, as they in ours, then we shall ourselves be debarred from true fulfilled existence.

MARTIN BUBER

Remember – we were told at Sinai, that you saw no shape or form of God. Not that it isn't there – but you did not see it. You only heard the Voice! Therefore, not having seen, you must make no image of God! You must feel God as a living, personal God, who goes forward. What stands still is dead. The gods that stood still, images, were only idols. God is a living God. He is always going ahead of man. And man must strive to follow Him, onward, higher. God always goes ahead. When man, in supreme ecstasy, does see God, he sees only His rearward parts. "Thou canst not see My face, for man shall not see Me and live". For then man would have seen everything. There would be no further striving left for him. Life is only in striving further. God is not in the past that has gone, nor in the present that stands still. "I am that I am!" God is always! God is the eternal future! And our striving to Him must be eternal!

I. L. PERETZ

How does a man find his Father who is in heaven? He finds Him by good deeds and the study of Torah. The Holy One, blessed be He finds man through love, brotherhood, truth, peace, humility, study; through a good heart; through a "no" that is a firm "no" and a "yes" that is a firm "yes".

SEDER ELIAHU RABBAH

The thread on which the different good qualities of human beings are strung as pearls, is the fear of God. When the fastenings of this fear are unloosed, the pearls roll in all directions and are lost one by one.

BOOK OF MORALS

RESPONSIBILITY – *Seeking the Hand of God*

If you had lived in the dread days of martyrdom, and the peoples had fallen on you to force you to apostatize from your faith, you would surely, as did so many, have given your life in its defence. Well then, fight now the fight laid on you in the better days, the fight with evil desire; fight and conquer, and seek for allies in this warfare of your soul, seek them in the fear of God and the study of the Torah. Forget not that God recompenses according to the measure with which you withstand the evil in your heart. Be a man in your youth; but if you were then defeated in the struggle, return, return at last to God, however old you may be.
ELEAZAR (ROKEACH) OF WORMS

O Lord, my whole desire is for You
Even though I cannot bring it to my lips.

When far from You, I die while yet in life;
But if I cling to You I live, though I should die.
JUDAH HALEVI

A man was going from village to village, everywhere asking the same question, "where can I find God?" He journeyed from Rabbi to Rabbi, and nowhere was he satisfied with the answers he received, so quickly he would pack his bags, and hurry on to the next village. Some of the Rabbis replied, "Pray, my son, and you shall find Him". But the man had tried to pray, and knew that he could not.
And some replied, "Study my child, and you shall find Him". But the more he read, the more confused he became, and the further he seemed from God.
And some replied, "Forget your quest, my child, God is within you". But the man had tried to find God within himself, and failed.
One day, the man arrived, very wearily, at a very small village set in the middle of an enormous forest. He went up to a woman who was minding some chickens, and she asked whom could he be looking for in such a small place, but she did not seem surprised when he told her that he was looking for God. She showed him to the Rabbi's house.
When he went in, the Rabbi was studying, so he waited a moment, but he was impatient to be off to the next village, if he could not be satisfied, so he interrupted, "Rabbi – how do I find God?"
The Rabbi paused, and the man wondered which of the many answers he had already received would he be told this time. But the Rabbi simply said, "You have come to the right place, my child. God is in this village. Why don't you stay a few days; you might meet Him".

RESPONSIBILITY – *Seeking the Hand of God*

The man was puzzled. He did not understand what the Rabbi could mean. But the answer was unusual, and so he stayed. For two or three days, he strode round and round, asking all the villagers where God was that morning, but they would only smile, and ask him to have a meal with them. Gradually, he got to know them, and even helped with some of the village work. Every now and then he would see the Rabbi by chance, and the Rabbi would ask him, "Have you met God yet, my son?"

And the man would smile, and sometimes he understood and sometimes he did not understand. For months he stayed in the village, and then for years. He became part of the village and shared in all its life. He went with the men to the synagogue on Friday and prayed with the rest of them, and sometimes he knew why he prayed, and sometimes he didn't. And sometimes he really said prayers, and sometimes only words. And then he would return with one of the men for a Friday night meal, and when they talked about God, he was always assured that God was in the village, though he wasn't quite sure where or when He could be found. Gradually, too, he began to believe that God was in the village, though he wasn't quite sure where. He knew, however, that sometimes he had met Him.

One day, for the first time, the Rabbi came to him and said, "You have met God now, have you not?"

And the man said, "Thank you, Rabbi, I think that I have. But I am not sure why I met Him, or how or when. And why is He in this village only?"

So the Rabbi replied, "God is not a person, my child, nor a thing. You cannot meet Him in that way. When you came to our village, you were so worried by your question that you could not recognize an answer when you heard it. Nor could you recognize God when you met Him, because you were not really looking for Him. Now that you have stopped persecuting God, you have found Him, and now you can return to your town if you wish".

So the man went back to his town, and God went with him. And the man enjoyed studying and praying, and he knew that God was within himself and within other people. And other people knew it too, and sometimes they would ask him, "Where can we find God?"

And the man would always answer, "You have come to the right spot: God is in this place".

JEFFREY NEWMAN

TRUTH

A "word" which I heard from him, (Rabbi Yechiel Yakob Weinberg), many years ago has been gaining more and more contemporary significance with every year that passes. I believe it was not his own. If I am not mistaken, he told it to us in the name of his teacher, Rabbi Nathan Zvi Finkel (Zecher Zaddik L'Vracha), the *Mashgiach* of Slobodka. It was based on the well-known Talmudical saying: "Jerusalem was destroyed because they based their words on the words of Torah". The Talmud, of course, asks the question: "But what else should they have done?" How can the basing of one's word on the Torah be considered a sin so grievous that, because of it Jerusalem was destroyed? The Talmud does give an answer. But the *Mashgiach* of Slobodka explained it differently. He emphasized the expression *divreihem* in the original. *Davar* is not only "word" in Hebrew, but also "thing", "interest", etc. *Divreihem* were their interests, matters that concerned them personally, their own affairs. The people of Jerusalem based their own personal interest on the words of the Torah; they justified their own selfish pursuits with the words of the Torah; they identified their own concerns with the concerns of the Torah. They said Torah, but meant themselves. This, explained Rabbi Weinberg, is the greatest of all sins; the falsification of the truth; the disguise of the lie in the garb of the truth. This is the greatest sin against the Torah. It well deserved the greatest punishment, the destruction of Jerusalem.
ELIEZER BERKOVITS

This age ... surprised by its tragedy, it longs for diversion, and catching itself in the act it looks for words.
KARL KRAUS

Absolutely!
When the Spring comes in and the sun is bright
Then every small blossom beckons and blows.
When the moon on her shining journey goes
Then stars swim after her through the night.
When the singer looks into two clear eyes
Then something is stirred and lyrics arise ...
But flowers and stars and songs just begun,
And moonbeams and eyes and the light of the sun,
No matter how much such stuff may please,
One can't keep living on things like these.
HEINRICH HEINE

TRUTH

It has become fashionable to talk of the relationship between God and man as that of a dialogue. That is as may be; but it should at least be noted that the dialogue involved is not a tea-table conversation. It is rather a call, even a calling to account; and it is curious to observe from the record how some of those called upon found in it terror and suffering and how some, for varying reasons, tried to evade it.
LEON ROTH

I have pointed out the error that threatens all young people and to which many fall prey: unable to withstand the impact of the divine (the unconditional) they evade it. But there exists still another, and more serious, error: the pretence of withstanding — a deception not only of others but of oneself ...
It may happen, by some odd perversity, that an individual entertains the illusion that he has surrendered himself to the divine whereas in fact he has evaded it: he interprets the fact of having been affected by the divine as having had an "experience". His being remains wholly unperturbed and unchanged, but he has savoured his hour of exaltation. He does not know the response; he knows only a "mood". He has psychologized God ...
In some way, religiosity may possibly penetrate the evaders but never the pretenders. One can be a rationalist, a freethinker, or an atheist in a religious sense, but one cannot, in a religious sense, be a collector of "experiences", a boaster of moods, or a prattler about God.
MARTIN BUBER

The soul when accustomed to superfluous things acquires a strong habit of desiring others which are necessary neither for the preservation of the individual nor for that of the species. This desire is without limit; whilst things which are necessary are few, and restricted within certain bounds. Lay this well to heart, reflect on it again and again; that which is superfluous is without end (and therefore the desire for it also without limit). Thus you desire to have your vessels of silver, but golden vessels are still better; others even have vessels studded with sapphires, emeralds, or rubies. Those, therefore, who are ignorant of this truth, that the desire for superfluous things is without limit, are constantly in trouble and pain. When they thus meet with the consequences of their course they complain of the judgments of God; they go so far as to say that God's power is insufficient, because He has given to this Universe the properties which they imagine cause these evils.
MAIMONIDES

TRUTH

A message is not the preaching of a preacher, but rather the man himself. He is the decisive element; only if he himself is a message can he bring a message. For only then will there go forth from him that reality which is conveyed in Dante's sentence: "he speaks reality, and you speak words". In the last analysis, therefore, only a pious man can preach. One speaks today frequently of "the affirmations of Judaism". The true affirmation of Judaism — that, is always the Jew himself, precisely he, who through himself becomes a message.

LEO BAECK

Hananiah (see *Jeremiah 28*) was a forthright patriot, and he was convinced that being patriotic meant being as he was. He was convinced that Jeremiah had no love whatsoever for his country, for if he had, how could he have expected his people to bend their necks to the yoke? But Jeremiah had a concrete concern for what was taking place. "Why should this city become desolate?" Hananiah had no such concern. Instead, he had his patriotism which does not allow such concerns to come up. What he called his fatherland was a political concept. Jeremiah's fatherland was a land inhabited by human beings, a settlement that was alive and mortal. His God did not wish it to perish. He wished to preserve it by putting those human beings under the yoke. Hananiah considered himself a great politician, for he thought that in an hour of danger he had succeeded in strengthening the people's resistance. But what he actually strengthened was an illusion, which when it collapsed would cause the collapse of the people's strength. Jeremiah, on the other hand, wanted to protect Israel from just that. The only way to salvation is by the steep and stony path over the recognition of reality. The feet of those who take it bleed, and there is always the threat of dizziness, but it is the one and only way.

The true prophets are the true politicians of reality, for they proclaim their political tidings from the viewpoint of the complete historical reality, which it is given them to see. The false prophets, the politicians who foster illusions, use the power of their wishful thinking to tear a scrap out of historical reality and sew it into their quilt of motley illusions. When they are out to influence through suggestion, they display the gay colours; and when they are asked for the material of truth, they point to the scrap, torn out of reality ...

False prophets are not godless. They adore the god "Success". They themselves are in constant need of success and achieve it promising it to the people. But they do honestly want success for the people. The craving for success governs their hearts and determines what rises from

TRUTH

them. That is what Jeremiah called "the deceit of their own heart". They do not deceive; they are deceived, and can breathe only in the air of deceit.

The true prophets know the little bloated idol which goes by the name of "Success" through and through. They know that ten successes that are nothing but successes can lead to defeat, while on the contrary ten failures can add up to a victory, provided the spirit stands firm. When true prophets address the people, they are usually unsuccessful; everything in the people which craves for success opposes them. But the moment they are thrown into the pit, whatever spirit is still alive in Israel bursts into flame, and the turning begins in secret which, in the midst of the deepest distress, will lead to renewal.

The false prophet feeds on dreams, and acts as if dreams were reality. The true prophet lives by the true word he hears, and must endure having it treated as though it only held true for some "ideological" sphere, "morals" or "religion", but not for the real life of the people.
MARTIN BUBER

The war is over and people have seen a lot of homes knocked down and now they don't feel safe in their own homes any more, in the way they used to feel safe and snug in them once. Something has happened that they can't get over and years will go by but they will never get over it. So we have lamps lit on our tables again and vases of flowers and portraits of our loved ones, but we don't believe in any of these things any more because once we had to abandon them without warning or scrape around pointlessly for them in the rubble ...

When you have been through it once, the experience of evil is never forgotten. Anybody who has seen homes knocked down knows only too well what fragile blessings vases of flowers and paintings and clean white walls are ... But we do not go defenceless against this fear. We have a toughness and resilience which others before us never knew ... We are forced to go on discovering an inner calm that is not born of carpets and vases of flowers.

There is no peace for the son of man. The foxes and the wolves have their lairs, but the son of man has no place to lay his head. Our generation is a generation of men. It is not a generation of foxes and wolves. There is not one of us who would not love to lay down his head somewhere, to have some snug, cosy little lair to creep into. But there is no peace for the sons of men. There is not one of us who at some time or other has not dreamed of being able to bed down on something soft and comfortable, be soothed, be master of some kind of certainty,

TRUTH

some faith or other, and rest. But now the old certainties have all been shattered, and faith has never been just a resting place. ... But we are bound to this anguish of ours and deep down glad of our destiny as men.
NATALIA GINZBURG (Turin 1946)

PURIFICATION

Purify our hearts to serve You in truth.
SHABBAT MORNING SERVICE

To him who wishes to defile himself, the doors are open; to him who wishes to purify himself, aid will be given.
SIMEON BEN LAKISH

Said the Besht: "When it is desired to solder a piece of silver to a silver vessel, the edge of the piece must be cleaned so that no foreign substance may intervene. Likewise when a man wishes to cleave to God, he must purify himself of every foreign thought beforehand.
CHASIDIC

On Yom Kippur Eve, Rabbi Schmelke said: "We are taught by the *Baraitha:* "Grains that have become unclean and are planted, become clean". Thus when the grain which came out of the ground is reunited with mother earth, its source, it becomes Levitically clean.
"Our souls come from God, and when they become unclean and impure, we may cleanse and purify them by returning them to their Source. Our souls must cleave entirely to the Fountain of Holiness. Then we may hope that the promise of the Lord may be fulfilled (*Deut 4:4*) 'But you that did cleave to the Lord, your God, are alive every one of you this day.'"
CHASIDIC

Purity of soul is an ethical concept. Nevertheless, let us not recoil from reading, in the third Book of Moses, the paragraphs that describe purification by the blood of sheep and doves as well as the great purification through the scapegoat. And when our hearts tremble under the impact of the great, ancient, but also alien, symbol, let us follow the way the people's soul took as it struggled for its purity, a way leading beyond prophets and psalmists to Akiba's liberating cry: "God is the purifying bath of Israel!" Only then will we become fully aware of the religious element in this concept of purity.
MARTIN BUBER

SIN – *Categories*

In Biblical Hebrew there are three main terms for sin – *pesha*, *avon* and *chet* ...

Pesha means rebellion. It refers to the attitude of mind through which a man sets himself up as the sole judge of his actions, recognizing neither God nor His law. *Pesha* signifies the refusal of man to consider himself accountable to God for his actions. For this type of man there are no external standards of right and wrong. Right is the name he gives to those actions which please him and further his aims, wrong, to those which displease him and frustrate his aims.

Avon comes from a root meaning "to be twisted", "to be crooked". It refers to the man whose course in life is deflected from the pursuit of the good ... It refers also to the twist in a man's character which seems to impel him to do wrong, to a queer perversity of temperament which propels him in the direction of wrong-doing ...

Chet is the weakest of the three terms. It comes from a root meaning "to miss". The word is used, for example, of an archer whose arrows fail to hit the target. *Chet* denotes failure to follow the good path, to the lack of character or staying power which prevents a man from arriving at the goal he has set himself ... Blame is attached even to unwitting sin if it could have been avoided with the exercise of greater care. The careless driver, the slack teacher, the over-indulgent or the neglectful parent, the thoughtless son, are all guilty of *chet*.
LOUIS JACOBS

SIN – *Free Will*

Free will is granted to every man. If he desires to incline towards the good way and be righteous, he has the power to do so; and if he desires to incline towards the unrighteous way and be a wicked man, he also has the power to do so. Give no place in your minds to that which is asserted by many of the ignorant: namely that the Holy One, blessed be He, desires that a man from his birth should be either righteous or wicked.

Since the power of doing good or evil is in our own hands, and since all the wicked deeds which we have committed have been committed with our full consciousness, it befits us to turn in penitence and to forsake our evil deed.
MAIMONIDES

SIN – *The Two Impulses*

"And God saw everything that He had made and, behold, it was very good". (*Genesis 1:31*) This refers to the two impulses in man, the good impulse and the impulse to evil. But is the impulse to evil "very good"? "Were it not for that impulse a man would not build a house, marry a wife, beget children or conduct business affairs".
GENESIS RABBAH

"Better is a poor and wise child than an old and foolish king". (*Eccles 4:13*) The first clause refers to the good impulse. Why is it called a child? Because it does not attach itself to a person until the age of thirteen and upward. Why is it called poor? Because all do not listen to it. Why is it called wise? Because it teaches creatures the right path. The second clause refers to the impulse to evil. Why does he call it a king? Because all listen to it. Why does he call it old? Because it attaches itself to a person from youth to old age. Why does he call it a fool? Because it teaches man the wrong path.
ECCLESIASTES RABBAH

The impulse to evil does not proceed along the sidewalks but in the middle of the highway. When it sees a man ogling with his eyes, straightening his hair and walking with a swaggering gait, it says, "This person belongs to me".
GENESIS RABBAH

The impulse to evil is at first like a spider's web, but in the end it is like cart-ropes.
SUCCAH

The impulse to evil is at first like a passer-by, then like a lodger, and finally like the master of the house.
SUCCAH

The impulse to evil is like one who runs about the world keeping his hand closed. Nobody knows what he has inside of it. He goes up to everyone and asks: "What do you suppose I have in my hand?" And every person thinks that just what he wants most of all is hidden there. And everyone runs after the impulse to evil. Then he opens his hand and it is empty.
CHASIDIC

SIN – *The Two Impulses*

Rabbi Shelomo asked: "What is the worst thing the impulse to evil can achieve?" And he answered: "To make man forget that he is the son of a king".
CHASIDIC

In the world to come the Holy One, blessed be He, will bring the impulse to evil and slay it in the presence of the righteous and wicked. To the righteous it will appear like a high mountain, to the wicked like a single hair. Both will weep. The righteous will weep and exclaim. "How were we able to subdue such a lofty mountain as this?" The wicked will weep and exclaim, "How were we unable to subdue a single hair like this?"
SUCCAH

If man sins because of his evil inclinations, he is misusing his *yetzer hara* and at the same time denying expression to his *yetzer tov*. By thus misdirecting and betraying his vital inclinations, man confounds himself. According to the Rabbis, a sin stupifies the human heart and defiles the soul. Every sin undermines a man's moral strength and diminishes his chances to meet the next temptation more hopefully. The Rabbis taught that a man's soul is the witness against him, whatever a man does, he does first of all to himself. A sin implies an act of self-defeat.
ELIEZER BERKOVITS

In the presence of their sleeping master, two disciples were talking about how hard it was to resist temptation, and how the *yetzer hara*, the Evil Desire, kept running after them. Their master, who had not been asleep after all, opened his eyes and said: "Don't flatter yourselves. The Evil Desire isn't running after you, you haven't reached that height. You're still running after the Evil Desire."
q. MILTON HIMMELFARB

It is because man is half angel, half brute, that his inner life witnesses such bitter war between such unlike natures. The brute in him clamours for sensual joy and things in which there is only vanity; but the angel resists and strives to make him know that meat, drink, sleep, are but means whereby the body may be made efficient for the study of the truths, and the doing of the will, of God. Not until the very hour of death can it be certain or known to what measure the victory has been won. He who is but a novice in the fear of God will do well to say audibly each day, as he rises: "This day I will be a faithful servant of the Almighty. I will be on my guard against wrath, falsehood, hatred, and quarrelsomeness, and will forgive those who wound me". For

SIN – *The Two Impulses*

whoso forgives is forgiven in his turn; hard-heartedness and a temper that will not make up quarrels are a heavy burden of sin. and unworthy of an Israelite.
MOSES OF COUCY

SIN – *Controlling the Impulse to Evil*

The wicked are under control of their heart (i.e. their impulse to evil), but the righteous have their heart under their control.
GENESIS RABBAH

When R. Yochanan ben Zakkai was on his death bed, his disciples came to visit him and before leaving they said: "Master, give us a farewell blessing". He said to them, "I pray that fearing God may be as important to you as fearing man". His disciples asked: "But should we not fear God more than man?" He replied, "If only you can attain this! When a man thinks of committing a transgression, he says: I hope no man sees me! If the fear of God is no more than this, it will be enough to keep you from many sins".
BERACHOT

A man should tell his teacher who teaches him God's ways, or even a trustworthy friend, all the evil thoughts he has which are in opposition to the holy Torah, which the impulse to evil brings into his head and heart, whether while he is studying the Torah or offering his prayers or when he lies in his bed or at any time during the day. He should conceal nothing out of shame. The result will be that by speaking of these matters, by bringing the potential to the actual, he will break the hold of the evil inclination so that it will have far less power to entice him on other occasions, quite apart from the sound spiritual guidance, which is the way of the Lord, that he may receive from his friend. This is a marvellous antidote to the impulse to evil.
ELIMELECH OF LIZENSK

If a man sees that his impulse to evil is gaining mastery over him, let him go to a place where he is unknown, put on black clothes and do what his heart desires; but let him not profane the Name publicly.
CHAGIGA

He who still harbours an impulse to evil has a great advantage, for he can serve God with it. He can gather all his passion and warmth and pour them into the service of God. He who has no impulse to evil at all cannot give perfect service. What counts is to restrain the blaze in the

SIN – Controlling the Impulse to Evil

hour of desire and let it flow into the hours of prayer and service.
CHASIDIC

What then is to be done with the "inclination of the heart"? One must teach it to respect the boundaries. Man is sufficiently free to acquire a high measure of control over his heart's inclination. "If you really want it, you can rule over it", says the Talmud (*Kiddushin 30b*).
Judaism has no illusion regarding man's difficulty in gaining control over the inclination of his heart. It is a never-ending struggle, and what is gained today may easily be lost tomorrow. As Rabbi Yitz'hak puts it, "The *yetzer* of a man renews itself daily against him" (*Kiddushin 30b*). Man may gain control over his evil inclination, but the next instant is a new moment and the beginning of a new struggle. Mastery over the evil inclination is never a condition which a man reaches; it is an event through which he passes, a station from which he has to move on to the next phase. "Do not trust yourself till the day of your death", says Hillel. (*Sayings of the Fathers 2:5*)
ELIEZER BERKOVITS

SIN – Its recognition

No sin is so light that it may be overlooked; no sin is so heavy that it may not be repented of.
M. IBN EZRA

Three sins no one can escape on any day: sinful thoughts, the presumption that God must answer our prayers, and dust of slander.
BABA BATHRA

Think not of the smallness of sin, but the greatness of Him against whom you have sinned.
BACHYA

R. Hoshaiah said: He who possesses knowledge, but has not the fear of sin, possesses nothing. Every craftsman who has no tools is no craftsman. The key which unlocks the Torah is the fear of sin.
EXODUS RABBAH

Sinners are mirrors. When we see faults in them, we must realize that they only reflect the evil in us.
BAAL SHEM

We hate the criminal and deal severely with him because we view in his deed, as in a distorting mirror, our own criminal instincts.
FREUD

SIN – *Its recognition*

R. Judah ben Tema used to say: Love and fear God; tremble and rejoice when you perform the commandments; if you have done a little wrong to your neighbour, let it seem to you large; if you have done him a big kindness, let it seem to you small; if he has done to you a big evil, let it seem to you small; if he has done to you a small kindness, let it seem to you large.
AVOT D'RABBI NATHAN

SIN – *Its effect*

Sin dulls the heart.
YOMA

A sin leaves a mark; repeated, it deepens the mark; when committed a third time, the mark becomes a stain.
ZOHAR

If one places in front of the window many thin and threadbare sheets, they have the same effect in screening the light of the sun as one heavy blanket. Similarly it is not only the serious sins which act as a screen between the Divine Light and the soul, but also the lesser offences, such as hiding oneself from the needs of the poor, indulging in slanderous talk, flying into a rage, pride and many such offences. Worst of all is the failure to engage in the study of the Torah.
SHNEOR ZALMAN OF LIADY

A man should always regard himself as though he were half guilty and half meritorious. If he performs one good deed, happy is he for weighting himself down in the scale of merit. If he commits one transgression, woe to him, for weighting himself down in the scale of guilt, for it is said, *but one sinner destroys much good* (*Eccles 9:18*) – on account of a single sin which he commits much good is lost him.
KIDDUSHIN

SIN – *Its antidote*

Consider three things and you will not come into the power of sin. Know what is above you – an eye that sees, an ear that hears, and that all your deeds are written in a book.
SAYINGS OF THE FATHERS

Akavya ben Mahalalel says, Keep three things in sight and you will not fall into the power of sin. Know where you come from, and where you go to, and before whom you are destined to give an account and reckoning.

SIN – *Its antidote*
SAYINGS OF THE FATHERS

If one guards himself against sin three times, the Holy One guards him from then on.
YERUSHALMI KIDDUSHIN

He who talks about and reflects on the evil he did, is thinking evil, and what one thinks, therein is one caught ... Stir filth this way or that, and it is still filth ... In the time I brood, I could be stringing pearls for the joy of heaven. This is what is written: "Depart from evil, and do good" (*Psalms 34:15*) – turn wholly from evil, do not brood over it, but do good. You have done wrong? Then balance it by doing right.
YITZHAK MEIR OF GER

There were once some highwaymen in the neighbourhood of R. Meir who caused him a lot of trouble. R. Meir prayed that they should die. His wife Beruriah said to him: "How do you conclude that such a prayer should be allowed?" "Because it is written, 'Let sins cease'". "Is it written 'sinners?' It is written 'sins!' Further, look at the end of the verse: 'and let the wicked men be no more'. (*Psalms 104:35*). Since the sins will cease, there will be no more wicked men! Rather pray for them that they should repent, and there will be no more wicked". He did pray for them, and they repented.
BERACHOT

SIN – *In Business Practice*

It is necessary to be most careful not to deceive one's neighbour. He who deceives his neighbour, whether it is the seller who deceives the buyer, or it is the buyer who deceives the seller, transgresses a prohibitory law, for it is written: "And when you sell anything to your neighbour, or when you buy anything from your neighbour, you shall not oppress one another". (*Lev 25:14*). And this is the first question that a man is asked when brought to judgment. "Did you transact your business honestly?"
Just as deception is forbidden in cases of buying and selling so is it prohibited with regard to hiring, contracts, or money changing.
If one has something to sell, he is forbidden to make it look better than what it really is in order to deceive thereby ...
It is likewise forbidden to mix a little bad food with plenty of good food to sell the same as though they were good, or to mix inferior liquor with superior liquor. But if the taste of the mixed wine be recognized, the mixing is permitted for the purchaser will detect it.

SIN – *In Business Practice*

A shopkeeper is permitted to give parched grain and nuts to children to accustom them to buy from him. He may also sell cheaper than the market price so that people buy from him and the other tradesmen cannot prevent this.

He who gives short measure or weight ... transgresses a prohibitory command of the Torah itself, for it is said: "You shall do no unrighteousness in your measures – of length, weight or capacity" (*Lev 19:35*). The punishment of short measures and weights is very severe, for the transgressor cannot repent properly as he does not know how and to whom to make restoration. Even if he institute public charities it is not considered a perfect repentance.

It is necessary to measure and to weigh with a generous eye ...

It is necessary to measure according to the customs of the country and no deviation therefrom is permitted ... For the Torah has laid down strict rules prohibiting incorrect measures lest a stumbling-block for others arise therefrom.

One who seeks to buy or rent property, be it real property, or chattels of a gentile or of an Israelite, if the price was agreed upon, although the sale was not yet completed, and some one else forestalled him and bought or rented it, the latter is called a wicked person. But if they had not yet agreed upon the price, for the seller asks so much and the buyer offers less, then some one else may buy it.

If one had made a deposit on a purchase or had marked the article for identification in the seller's presence, or if the seller said to him, "Mark your purchase", even though he did not hereby acquire title to that article, nevertheless, if one retracts, be he the buyer or the seller, he does not act as becomes an Israelite, and he incurs Divine punishment. It is proper to abide by one's word even though he neither paid anything on account, nor did he put a mark upon the article, nor was the purchase completed; even if they merely agreed upon a price, neither of them may retract his agreement. He who retracts, be he the buyer or the seller, is considered to be one lacking honesty, and the spirit of our Sages finds no pleasure in him, for it is proper for an Israelite to abide by his word ... Furthermore it is the duty of the perfect to fulfill even the thoughts in his heart; thus if he thought and came to the conclusion that he would sell a certain article at a certain price, and the purchaser, not aware of it, offered him more, he shall only take that amount at which he had his mind made up to sell it to him, so that he fulfill what is written: "And speaks the truth in his heart" (*Psalms 15:2*) ... This applies also to similar matters, appertaining to dealings between man and man, that he must fulfill his thoughts, e.g. he should not alter his

SIN – In Business Practice

determinations if he is able to do it. But whatever relates to one's own needs, he is not bound to fulfill even what proceeds from his mouth, as long as no performance of a precept is involved therein.

If one promised a small gift to his neighbour, who depended upon it, being sure that he would give it to him, if he retract his promise and fail to give it, he is likewise one of those who lack honesty ... Even if he did not utter the promise but he only determined in his heart that he would give, he must fulfill his intention;

KITZUR SHULCHAN ARUCH

SIN – Of Pride

Pride means that a man thinks highly of himself and imagines that he deserves to be praised. There may be a number of reasons for him so thinking. One man thinks he is intelligent, another that he is handsome, another that he has dignity, another that he is a great man, another that he is wise. The general principle is this. Whenever a man imagines that he has any of the virtues he is in immediate danger of falling into the trap of pride ...

There is the proud man who thinks to himself that since he is worthy of praise and is, in his own esteem, unique and outstanding, it is proper for him to behave in a special way and conduct himself with great dignity when he walks, when he sits or stands, when he opens his mouth and in whatever he does. He walks slowly and leisurely, step by step. He sits upright. He rises gradually as the snake raises its head. He refuses to converse with just anybody but only with the gentry and even then he will only utter a few words as if an oracle were speaking. He will be pompous in all that he does, in his movements, his eating and drinking, his dressing and in all his ways, as if his flesh were lead and his bones stone or sand.

Another proud man imagines that since he is worthy of praise and has so many good qualities it is necessary for him to make the whole earth tremble at his presence and be terrified of him ...

Another proud man imagines himself to be so great and so full of dignity that he thinks it quite impossible for him to lose the respect of others and he thinks that he does not need it ...

Another proud man wants to be so singled out for his virtues and so distinguished in his conduct that it is not enough for him that everyone should praise him for all the other virtues he imagines he possesses but he wants them to praise him, too, for his humility, that he is the most modest of men. This man takes pride in his humility and seeks fame by

SIN — *Of Pride*

appearing to run away from it. Such a man will be ready to place himself below people who are really inferior to him and even below the most unworthy because he imagines that in so doing he demonstrates how perfectly humble he really is ...

Finally there are other proud men whose pride is kept hidden within themselves so that it never shows. But in their hearts they imagine that they are already very wise and know the truth about everything and that few can be so clever. They consequently have no regard for any opinions other than their own, thinking to themselves that anything they find difficult cannot possibly be easy for others ...

All these are examples of the results of pride which sets back the wise and makes them foolish. Pride distracts the wisest of men, how much more young pupils who have not served their apprenticeship properly ... Anyone who wants to acquire the quality of cleanness must cleanse himself of all of these. One should appreciate that pride is nothing more than a form of blindness in which a man cannot see his faults and admit his inferiority. For if he were able to see and to recognize the truth he would depart as far as he could from these crooked and perverse ways.
MOSES CHAIM LUZZATTO

SIN — *Of Anger*

Bear in mind that life is short, and that with every passing day you are nearer to the end of your life. Hence how can you waste your time on petty quarrels and family discords. Restrain your anger; hold your temper in check, and enjoy peace with everyone.
NACHMAN OF BRATZLAV

Rabbi Menachem Mendel of Lubavitch used to restrain an angry outburst until he had looked into the codes to learn whether anger is permissible in the particular instance. But how much genuine anger could he feel after searching for the authority in the *Shulchan Aruch*!
CHASIDIC

When a man quarrels with you, do not imitate him, for then your opponent will discover that he spoke the truth about you. Revenge yourself through kind deeds toward him, and it will be proved that he lied.
NACHMAN OF BRATZLAV

SIN — *Of Prejudice*

As soon as I had said it I was sorry. By using the German word I had

SIN – *Of Prejudice*

tried to humiliate him. My desire to humiliate this young man was causing me to feel guilty, and yet at the same time I asked myself why I should feel hurt for wanting to hurt the German. Then it occurred to me that this was the argument of the S.S.; to hurt, to kill the Jew is not a sin; it is an act of delousing. The feelings I was experiencing were not my own feelings, but theirs. I felt confused. I was doing to him what they had done to me. I was persecuting an innocent man whose only sin was that he happened to be born in Germany.

EUGENE HEIMLER

SIN – *Of "Slander"*

There are six types of evil talkers.

The first is the man who finds faults with others when they have no faults, and sometimes blames those who are not only innocent of the fault but are worthy people. Such a person embraces both the evils of falsehood and slander ... You should know that whoever agrees with a slanderous statement when he hears it is as bad as the one who utters it, for everyone will say that the report must be true since those who heard it agreed with it.

The second type is the man who speaks evil of others but is careful not to say anything that is untrue ... Whoever repeats evil things about others does two evils. First he causes harm to others and brings disgrace upon them. Secondly, he demonstrates that he is pleased to be able to blame others and to rejoice in their downfall ... However in matters where the happiness of other human beings is at stake, for instance, in cases of theft, oppression, assault, causing others pain or putting them to shame, or wronging others, it is permitted for the person who witnessed the offense to repeat it to others in order to help the victim and be zealous for the truth.

The third type is the talebearer ... There are no limits to the harm done by the talebearer for he adds to hatred in the world ... Greater than any other offense of evil talk is when one stirs up trouble between brothers and friends, causing them to hate one another ...

The fourth type is the *dust* of evil talk ... which is the term used for a man who speaks words which bring others to speak evil ... Suppose a woman asks her neighbour for fire and she replies: Where is fire to be found if not in the house of so-and-so where they are always roasting meat to eat? ... A man is obliged to take care that when he speaks no one will suspect him of having the intention of speaking evil.

The fifth type is unclean talk.

SIN – Of "Slander"

The sixth type is the complainer. The complainer is the man who is always grumbling and whining and finding fault with his friend's conduct and speech even though the friend is quite innocent of any desire to harm him. Such a person always finds reason for accusing, never for excusing. He treats every unintentional slight as if it were intentional. He imagines himself to be victimized and is full of his neighbour's sins against him whereas in reality he is the offender ... Keep yourself, therefore, far from the way of the complainers for they harm only themselves and know not of peace. Teach your tongue to find excuses for others and let your loins be girded with righteousness.
JONAH BEN ABRAHAM GERONDI

SIN – Of "Flattery"

The first category consists of those flatterers who recognize, see, or know of some wrong practice of their neighbour's and of his abiding by deceit, or of one man's sinning against another through slander or through injurious words – and who smooth over his offenses with an evil tongue saying, "You have committed no wrong" ... This foolish flatterer is guilty of a grave transgression, for he is not jealous of truth, but abets falsehood; he calls what is bad, good and turns darkness to light ...

The second category consists of those who flatter the evildoer before others, whether or not in his presence, even though they do not justify his crime or give a false account of him, but simply say that he is a good man ... for his mentioning the good and not the evil, and concealing his offenses, will cause the hearers to regard him as a righteous man and to accord him honour, thus strengthening his hand ...

The third category consists of those who praise the evildoer to his face, but who are guided by wisdom to the extent that they do not praise him in the presence of others, lest their doing so prove to be a stumbling block. The transgression of these flatterers, too, is a great one, for because of their "sugar-coating" of him, he will not turn from his evil path, and his transgressions will cause him no anxiety, for he will be righteous in his eyes ...

The fourth category consists of those who befriend the evildoer ...

The fifth category consists of those whose words are trusted by others and upon whose words all who hear them rely – who form the intention of elevating one among the people or one of their close relatives, out of affection for him, and who say about him that he is a wise man, when he is actually not wise, so that he becomes a hindrance

SIN – *Of "Flattery"*

and a stumbling-block; for his directions will be relied upon, and he will decide all disputes, pervert judgment and produce chaos ...

The sixth category consists of those who are in a position to protest, but do not do so, in whose mouths there is no rebuke, who do not sharpen their eyes against evil deeds, nor pay heed to them, and who do not reprove others, in spite of our having been commanded to remove the evil from our people's midst ...

The seventh category consists of those who see the people of their place to be stiff-necked, but who say in their hearts, "Perhaps they will not listen if I tell them the truth and fill my mouth with rebuke" ... Perhaps if he had bestirred their spirits, they would have awakened from the sleep of their foolishness and their error would not have remained with them ...

The eighth category consists of those who hear the words of slanderers, or who hear every mouth speaking foulness, or who sit in the midst of scoffers who shame Torah and *mitzvoth* and ... hold their tongues ...

The ninth category consists of those who give honour to the wicked by way of courtesy ... The only reason for which it is permitted to honour the wicked is the fear of their causing injury or loss when their hand is strong and the times favour their audacity so that it is not within our hands to humble them, nor within our power to move them from their place ...

JONAH BEN ABRAHAM GERONDI

SIN – *Of Religion*

Religion has become a substitute for the couch of the psychoanalyst. It is expected to give us peace of mind, to bring us happiness, to guarantee us good health, and to assure us of never-ending prosperity. This religion is not God oriented but man centered; man is not required to serve God, but God is meant to serve man. It is the typical religion of a comfortable middle class. We have everything now: jobs, professions, homes, cars, insurance policies; and we also have a God. It is useful to have a God; one can never tell when one may need Him. Our religion is a prop for our prosperity and comforts. No one is concerned with the word of God; no one listens and no one obeys. The function of our awakened piety is to confirm us in our habits and our customary way of thought. We believe in God, but we also limit His authority. We prescribe for Him how to act toward us. Truth for Him is what *we* hold to be true; right what *we* consider right. He can ask of us no more than what we ask of ourselves. Most important of all, He is to be considerate; in no way may He inconvenience us or interfere with our comforts and pleasures.

ELIEZER BERKOVITS

SIN – *Of Religion*

R. Abun erected two grand gates for the House of Study, and he showed them to R. Mina. The latter Rabbi quoted *Hosea 8:14*. "Israel builds temples, and forgets his Maker", and went on to say, "Had you spent this money more piously, would there not have been many labouring in the Torah?"

YERUSHALMI SHEKALIM

I am not intending to tread on anyone's corns. It is not considered advisable nowadays to stress the differences between Orthodox, Conservative, and Reform Jews, and their respective virtues and faults. But there is one danger against which they must all guard – the danger of becoming a bore. Being a bore is perhaps the worst offense possible in religious life. When Satan wants to destroy religious life he sends it a bore, to make the people yawn. And nothing that is done with methods that are outside religion will help to put things right. A congregational dance or a concert or a lecture on a subject that is not itself religious will not expel the religious boredom once it has got there. It doesn't add anything more to religious feeling in the congregation. I am not against a dance or a concert or a lecture. I believe they can all fulfil a religious function, if there is religion in the centre of it, and all these other functions are irradiated by religion. Religion can't by its nature be a side issue. Either it is central, with everything else subservient, consciously or unconsciously, or it is no longer religion. It can't live in a corner. If it tries to do that the time will soon come when it is swept out from the corner and thrown on the dust heap.

CHAIM GREENBERG

The author of *"Kol Omer Kera"* said: "We read in a *Midrash* that Cain and Abel quarrelled for the reason that each wished to establish the Holy Temple on his land. This excuse has been used ever since for every shedding of blood and for every war. People always say that they fight on behalf of a holy purpose."

CHASIDIC

Religious experience is both the source and the end of what is usually called religion. Originally religion is the web of complex attempts at communicating the incommunicable. For religious experience, like all experience and by definition, is personal, subjective. In as far as it really is a religious experience i.e. more than an emotional wallop, it is powerful, sometimes overwhelming, always incontrovertible. I see, I hear, I know. There is no doubt that it has happened to me, that it has pulled the world or at least my soul together. It has wholed me, healed me, "saved" me. It has given me a new "end", has redirected my steps,

SIN – Of Religion

has given me the chance of *metanoia*, repentance, of what the prophets called "turning from death to life" ...

Isaiah "saw" the Lord, "high and lifted up" and the whole earth as reflecting his glory with only man refusing to play his part and destroying his social and personal reality or integrity by such a refusal ... When Isaiah "had seen", he heard the question: "Whom shall we send?" And naturally the seer says: "Send me". And though it be ten times over useless, he will be sent. Because of its conviction and self-evidence, and because of its revelation of glory, or glorious possibilities, the vision demands to be communicated. It must be expressed in word and action. It calls for total committal and response. It makes the visionary feel responsible for others. He is the watchman from whose hand the blood of his brothers will be required, unless he has warned them in time ...

Religious experience is personal. Religion remains meaningless, until it has become a personal experience. In religion words, doctrines, laws, traditions, conventions, liturgies, can never be more than pointers, hints, suggestions, introductions. What matters is that which is left when the word has been spoken, the music faded, the picture vanished. In religion we could become aware, even more intensely than in art, of a simple psychic fact: That much of what seems to matter most in the everyday world of human struggle is quite immaterial as far as the *quality* of personal experience is concerned. Yet what matters more in heaven or on earth than this quality? Upset the balance of the soul or psyche ever so little and the world turns to dust and ashes ...

Now it seems to me that religion becomes daemonic, destructive and, most of all, self-destructive, that it begins to lower the quality of experience, when it becomes dogmatic, traditional, conventional, when it mistakes its formulations for the experience they are merely intended to point at. As Jeremiah already knew: All is lost when we begin to say "this is the temple of the Lord, this is the temple of the Lord, this is ..."

WERNER PELZ

In my earlier years the "religious" was for me the exception ... "Religious experience" was the experience of an otherness which did not fit into the context of life ... The "religious" lifted you out. Over there now lay the accustomed existence with its affairs, but here illumination and ecstasy and rapture held, without time or sequence ... The illegitimacy of such a division of the temporal life ... was brought home to me by an everyday event, an event of judgment ...

What happened was no more than that one forenoon, after a morning of "religious" enthusiasm, I had a visit from an unknown young man,

SIN – *Of Religion*

without being there in spirit. I certainly did not fail to let the meeting be friendly, I did not treat him any more remissly than all his contemporaries who were in the habit of seeking me out about this time of day as an oracle that is ready to listen to reason. I conversed attentively and openly with him — only I omitted to guess the questions which he did not put. Later, not long after, I learned from one of his friends — he himself was no longer alive — the essential content of these questions; I learned that he had come to me not casually, but borne by destiny, not for a chat but for a decision. He had come to me, he had come in this hour. What do we expect when we are in despair and yet go to a man? Surely a presence by means of which we are told that nevertheless there is meaning.

MARTIN BUBER

On November 10, 1938, the Nazis celebrated what in their never-never language they called Crystal Night. During the black hours of that night, they burned or demolished stone by stone every Synagogue in Germany. A week or so later we at (Temple) Beth El decided to have a service of grief and sorrow for the Synagogues that were destroyed. To the special service we invited all Jewish refugees in Providence (Rhode Island). On that Friday night, about ten minutes before the service was to begin, a man then active in the Congregation rushed into the little room at the rear of the Temple where I sat: "Did you give permission to these people to wear hats?" The fact was that until that instant I had given no thought to the headgear of our guests — the refugees. I did not know whether or not our guests chose to wear hats, to put on *Yarmulkes*, or not to wear either. And so my response to the question which sounded to me like "When did you stop beating your Mother?" was indirect. I began to say: "But these people are our guests. They have suffered so much. Whether or not they choose to wear their hats, surely we do not wish to add insult to the injuries they had already suffered." But my interrogator was implacable. "Answer my question. Did you or did you not give permission to these people to wear their hats?" To this day, I don't know the outcome of the battle of the hats. I was too choked up with pain. Involuntarily I thought of comparable demands — of Cossack officers saying to Jews "Shapka doloi", "Off with your hat", of SS men saying, "Hut ab, Jude". So when I walked into the Temple I did not look. My head was reeling; my eyes were filled with tears. To this day I do not know whether ushers took it upon themselves to tell our guests to remove their hats and whether some of the refugees left in protest. Whatever happened to the hats worn by our guests, that service for me at least was indeed a service of grief and sorrow.

WILLIAM G. BRAUDE

CHESHBON HANEFESH – *Self-Judgment*

When your life is tumbling downhill head over heels,
Thrashing and foaming like an epileptic,
Don't pray and offer up repentance,
Don't be afraid of jail and ruin.

Study your past with concentration,
Evaluate your days without self-flattery,
Grind the fag-ends of illusions underfoot,
But open up to all that's bright and clear.

Don't surrender to impotence and bitterness,
Don't give in to disbelief and lies,
Not everyone's a cringing bastard,
Not everyone's a bigot who informs.

And while you walk along the alien roads
To lands which do not figure on your maps,
Count out the names of all your friends
As you would do with pearls or prayer-beads.

Be on the look-out, cheerful and ferocious,
And you'll manage to stand up, yes, stand up
Under your many-layered load of misery,
Under the burden of your being right.

YULI DANIEL (WRITTEN IN A SOVIET LABOUR CAMP)

When I was eleven years of age, spending the summer on my grandparents' estate, I used, as often as I could do it unobserved, to steal into the stable and gently stroke the neck of my darling, a broad dapple-grey horse. It was not a casual delight but a great, certainly friendly, but also deeply stirring happening. If I am to explain it now, beginning from the still very fresh memory of my hand, I must say that what I experienced in touch with the animal was the Other, the immense otherness of the Other, which, however, did not remain strange like the otherness of the ox and the ram, but rather let me draw near and touch it. When I stroked the mighty mane, sometimes marvellously smooth-combed, at other times just as astonishingly wild, and felt the life beneath my hand, it was as though the element of vitality itself bordered on my skin, something that was not I, was certainly not akin to me, palpably the other, not just another, really the Other itself; and yet it let me approach, confided itself to me, placed itself elementally in the relation of *Thou* and *Thou* with me. The horse, even when I had not begun by

CHESHBON HANEFESH – *Self-Judgment*

pouring oats for him into the manger, very gently raised his massive head, ears flicking, then snorted quietly, as a conspirator gives a signal meant to be recognizable only by his fellow-conspirator; and I was approved. But once — I do not know what came over the child, at any rate it was childlike enough — it struck me about the stroking, what fun it gave me, and suddenly I became conscious of my hand. The game went on as before, but something had changed, it was no longer the same thing. And the next day, after giving him a rich feed, when I stroked my friend's head he did not raise his head. A few years later, when I thought back to the incident, I no longer supposed that the animal had noticed my defection. But at the time I considered myself judged.
MARTIN BUBER

JUDGMENT

If there is no judgment (below) there is judgment (above).
ELEAZAR BEN PEDAT

The world is judged by the majority of its people, and an individual by the majority of his deeds. Happy is he who performs a good deed: that may tip the scale for him and the world.
ELEAZAR B. SIMEON

The horn blown on the New Year's Day at the peak of the festival stamps the day as a "day of judgment". The judgment usually thought of as at the end of time is here placed in the immediate present ... Every individual is meted out his destiny according to his actions. The verdict for the past and the coming year is written on New Year's Day, and it is sealed on the Day of Atonement, when the last reprieve constituted by these ten days of penitence and turning to God is over. The year becomes representative of eternity, in complete representation. In the annual return of this day of judgment, eternity is stripped of every trace of the beyond, of every vestige of remoteness; it is actually there within the grasp of every individual and holding every individual close in its strong grasp. He is no longer part of the eternal history of the eternal people, nor is he part of the eternally changing history of the world. There is no more waiting, no more hiding behind history.
FRANZ ROSENZWEIG

He who desires to become aware of the hidden light must lift the feeling of fear up to its source. And he can accomplish this if he judges himself and all he does. For then he sheds all fears and lifts fear that has

JUDGMENT

fallen down. But if he does not judge himself, he will be judged from on high, and this judgment will come upon him in the guise of countless things, and all the things in the world will become messengers of God who carry out the judgment on this man.

CHASIDIC

The thought that man has constantly to examine himself before, and confess to, his God makes evident the impossibility of attaining the ideal. In his freedom man stands before the omnipresent and omniscient God who is the "judge of all the earth" (*Genesis 18:25*) and "who regards no person and takes no bribe" (*Deut 10:17*). The Eternal "searches the heart and tries the reins, even to give every man according to his ways, and according to the fruit of his doings" (*Jeremiah 17:10*). "Where could I go from Your spirit, or where could I flee from Your presence?" (*Psalms 139:7*). This thought is similarly expressed in rabbinic literature: "You are judged every day". "Know what is above you: an eye that sees, an ear that hears, and that all your deeds are written in a book". "He is God, He is the Fashioner, He is the Creator. He knows; He is Judge, He is Witness, He is Accuser; He will judge". Birth and death remind us of this judgment: "Know where you come from, and where you go to, and before whom you are destined to give an account and reckoning". To believe that there is "no judgment and no judge" is viewed as the root of all sin. This idea of responsibility before God has become the sermon for the New Year's Day, which has become known as the "Day of Judgment", the day on which our soul feels again the need to confess to God.

LEO BAECK

Believe not that the world is for naught, made
For the wolf and the fox, for murd'rer and cheat;
That the sky is a blind to keep God from perceiving
The fog that thy hands not be seen
And the wind just to drown bitter wails.
The world is not hovel, market or cast-off.

All will be measured, all will be weighed
Not a fear nor a blood drop will fade,
Nor the spark in one soul be extinguished uncharged.
Tears gather in streams, and streams into oceans,
Oceans will swell to a flood.
And sparks burst into thunder ...
Oh, think not there is no judgment or judge!

I. L. PERETZ

JUDGMENT AND MERCY

Rosh Hashanah is a day of judgment with mercy and Yom Kippur is a day of mercy with judgment.
NACHMANIDES

The sinner himself is to turn to God, since it is he who turned away. It was his sin and it must be his conversion. No one can substitute for him in his return, no one can atone for him; no one stands between him and God, no mediator or past event, no redeemer and no sacrament. He must purify himself, he must attain his own freedom, for he was responsible for his loss of it. Faith and trust alone are therefore not sufficient; nor does confidence in God or a reliance upon an already acquired salvation suffice. Here again it is the deed which is paramount. Atonement is ours; it is our task and our way.
LEO BAECK

TESHUVAH — *Repentance*

Seven things were created before the Universe came into being. They are Torah, repentance, Paradise, Gehinnom, the Throne of Glory, the Sanctuary and the name of the Messiah.
PESACHIM

The gates of prayer are sometimes open and sometimes closed, but the gates of repentance are ever open. As the sea is always accessible, so is the hand of the Holy One, blessed be He, always open to receive penitents.
DEUTERONOMY RABBAH

The prayer for Understanding is first (in the Eighteen Benedictions), for it is intellect that brings man near to God, and the prayer of Repentance follows immediately to teach us that our Understanding should be applied to His Torah and service.
JUDAH HALEVI

It is written: "Good and upright is the Lord, therefore He will instruct sinners in the way". (*Psalms 25:8*). They asked Wisdom, "What shall be the punishment of the sinner?" Wisdom answered, "Evil pursues sinners" (*Proverbs 13:21*). They asked Prophecy. It replied, "The soul that sins it shall die" (*Ezekiel 18:4*). They asked the Torah. It replied, "Let him bring a sacrifice" (*Lev 1:4*). They asked God, and He replied "Let him repent, and obtain his atonement. My children, what do I ask of you? Seek Me and live".
PESIKTA D' RAV KAHANA

TESHUVAH — *Repentance*

Rab said: Whoever commits a transgression and is filled with shame because of it, all his sins are forgiven him.

BERACHOT

Teshuvah, return, is the name given to the act of decision in its ultimate intensification; it denotes the decisive turning point in a man's life, the renewing, total reversal in the midst of the normal course of his existence. When in the midst of "sin", that is, in decisionlessness, the will to decision awakens, the cover of routine life bursts open, and primal forces break through, storming heavenward. In the man who returns, creation begins anew; in his renewal the substance of the world is renewed.

MARTIN BUBER

Psalms

Happy is the man whom thou hast set apart
For chastisement and then hast healed his heart.

Happy is the man that saith: I trust
and praise the hand that rolls my pride in dust.

Happy is the man that saith: In burst
Of anger once I hated and I curst.
This curse upon me left a lasting stain,
And ranking hatred proved my sorest bane,
Until I drank my fill of galling woe,
And then my heart was cleansed as pure as snow.

Happy is the man that saith: relieve
Me of my haughty mind and grant reprieve,

And he that saith: The world is fair to see;
If it seem ill, the evil bides in me.

Happy is the man that saith; Above
All earthly might and fame I crave love.
Would that the words my heart and lips express
Were balm for wounds, to soothe and heal and bless.
Would that my eyes would shine and send forth light,
To be a beacon in another's night.

YEHOASH

TESHUVAH — *Conscience*

"The spirit of man is the lamp of God, searching all the inward parts" (*Proverbs 20:27*). The "lamp of God" is the human conscience, which

TESHUVAH — *Conscience*

sharply distinguishes man from other creatures. Periodically our conscience makes us painfully aware of the distance between our conduct and our ideal self, that self which enables us to believe that man is made in the divine image. We are born into the world with the freedom to choose between servitude to the material world or service to God ... The unrepentant sinner readily and easily forgives himself; the repentant person prays fervently with the psalmist: "Create me a clean heart and renew a steadfast spirit within me", (*Psalms 51:12*). If he fortifies this prayer with a resolute will, he will succeed in building a nobler life upon the ruins of the old.

MAX ARZT

To knock timidly at distant gates of silence, inquiring whether there is a God somewhere, is not the way. We all have the power to discover in the nearest stone or tree, sound or thought, the shelter of His often desecrated goodness.

ABRAHAM JOSHUA HESCHEL

TESHUVAH — *Meaning*

Previous to repentance a man has no real existence, and it were better for him not to have been born; it is repentance which gives him existence. By repentance he declares: "I am ready to exist as a man of worth".

After repentance a man understands God better, and he knows that his repentance was performed in the light of his lack of understanding; hence he must repent again in the light of his greater understanding. Again he attains higher understanding, which leads him to repent once more. Hence there is no limit to penitence. For this reason we pray day after day three times: Bring us back in perfect repentance to Your presence. Blessed are You Lord, who desires repentance.

NACHMAN OF BRATZLAV

Rabbi Zussya of Hanipol said: "There are five verse in the Bible which constitute the essence of Judaism. These verses begin in Hebrew with one of these letters: 'Tav, Shin, Vav, Beth, Heh', which comprise the Hebrew word for Repentance: 'Teshuvah'.

1. You shall be whole-hearted with the Lord, your God. (*Deut 18:13*)
2. I have set the Lord always before me. (*Psalms 16:8*)
3. But you shall love your neighbour as yourself. (*Lev 19:18*)
4. In all your ways acknowledge Him. (*Proverbs 3:6*)
5. To walk humbly with your God. (*Micah 6:8*)

"Therefore, resolve to act accordingly, so that your repentance may be sincere".

CHASIDIC

TESHUVAH — *Turning about*

The repentant sinner should strive to do good with the same faculties with which he sinned. If, for instance, his tongue gave offence to others, he should study the Torah aloud. With whatever part of the body he sinned he should now engage in good deeds. If the feet had run to sin let them now run to the performance of the good. The mouth that had spoken falsehood should be opened in wisdom. Violent hands should now open in charity. The haughty eye should now gaze downwards. The plotting heart should now meditate on the teachings of Torah. The trouble-maker should now become a peace-maker.
JONAH BEN ABRAHAM GERONDI

A *chasid* complained to Rabbi Zev Wolf of Zbarazh that certain persons were turning night into day, playing cards. "That is good", said the *zaddik*. "Like all people, they want to serve God and don't know how. But now they are learning to stay awake and persist in doing something. When they have become perfect in this, all they need do is turn to God — and what excellent servants they will make for Him then!"
CHASIDIC

All is God's

Man has separated lust and sorrow.
But God holds them together like day and night.
I know lust. I know intense suffering.
I praise God's one name.

God's Gifts

My most pious songs have I written
On rising from my sinful bed.
God has given me a wealth of sins,
And God alone has saved me from my sins.
JACOB ISRAEL DE HAAN

TESHUVAH — *Its power*

Neither sin-offering nor trespass-offering nor death nor the Day of Atonement can bring expiation without repentance.
TOSEFTA YOMA

Repentance makes man a new creature; hitherto, dead through sin, he is fashioned afresh.
MIDRASH PSALMS

TESHUVAH – *Its power*

Man stands before God, yet how can he stand before God? This is the decisive question of faith that here arises. True, there is in us the divine and the real; but does not our sin separate us from the source of the divine and the real? True, we are the children of God; but do we cease to be so if godlessness – that is sin – takes hold of us? Our soul is pure, but can it not become unclean if it becomes unfree and subjects itself to the evil and destructive? Is there not then opened a cleft between God and man, so that there is no longer a path from man to God and from God to man? The answer to these questions attained by the Jewish soul is the conviction that the conflict can be surmounted by means of the "return" (*Teshuvah*) and its atonement, which return brings about. Man can "return" to his freedom and purity, to God, the reality of his life. If he has sinned, he is always able to turn and to find his way back to the holy, which is more than the earthly and beyond the limitations of his life; he can hallow and purify himself again; he can atone. He can always decide anew and begin anew. For man there is always the constant possibility of a new ethical beginning. The task of choice and realization, of freedom and deed, is never completed. "Return!" – thus does Judaism speak to men so long as they breathe; "return" – but not as misunderstanding has interpreted it, "do penance". This return, this *Teshuvah*, is the atonement of which man is never bereft and in which he is always able to renew his life. "Return one day before your death".
LEO BAECK

The past can be cancelled by a true cry from the heart to God and a return to His law. This holds not only for the annual reckoning, but to the last hour a man lives; so my grandfather taught me.
He had in his Bronx apartment a lodger less learned than himself, and much fiercer in piety. One day when we were studying the laws of repentance together, the lodger burst from his room. "What!" he said. "The atheist guzzles whisky and eats pork and wallows with his women all his life long, and then repents the day before he dies and stands guiltless? While I spend a lifetime trying to please God?" My grandfather pointed to the book. "So it is written," he said gently. – "Written!" the lodger roared. "There are books and there are books." And he slammed back into his room.
The lodger's outrage seemed highly logical. My grandfather pointed out afterwards that cancelling the past does not turn it into a record of achievement. It leaves it blank, a waste of spilled years. A man had better return, he said, while time remains to write a life worth scanning. And since no man knows his death day, the time to get a grip on his life is the first hour when the impulse strikes him.
HERMAN WOUK

TESHUVAH — *Between man and man*

R. Josiah on *Zephaniah 2:1*. "Correct yourselves". First, let us correct *ourselves*, then only let us seek to correct others.
LAMENTATIONS RABBAH

In the neighbourhood of R. Ze'era there lived some coarse men, but he drew near them so that they might repent. His colleagues, the Rabbis were angry with him. When R. Ze'era died, the men said, "Till now we had R. Ze'era who besought compassion for us; who will do so now?" They pondered upon this in their hearts and repented.
SANHEDRIN

Let not a man, after he has sinned, say "There is no restoration for me," but let him trust in the Lord and repent, and God will receive him. Let him not say, "If I confess, I shall lose my office", but let him hate office, and humble himself, and return in repentance.
MIDRASH PSALMS

If a wicked man abandons his wickedness and repents, do not despise him.
MIDRASH PROVERBS

It is a flagrant sin to say to a repentant person: Remember your past deeds; or to mention them in his presence so as to embarrass him, or to recall similar incidents that are reminiscent of what he did. All this is forbidden along with all kinds of insulting words against which Torah warns us, as it is written: "You must not vex one another".
MAIMONIDES

When Akavya ben Mahalalel was dying, his son said to him: "Father commend me to some of your comrades". Akavya replied: "I will not commend you". His son said to him: "Is it because of some fault you have found in me?" He answered: "No. But your deeds will endear you, and your deeds will estrange you".
MISHNAH EDUYOT

TESHUVAH — *Forgiving Others*

Forgive your neighbour his wrongdoing;
That your sins will be forgiven when you pray.
Shall one man cherish anger against another,
And yet ask healing from the Lord?
Does he have no mercy on a man like himself,
And yet pray for his own sins?
BEN SIRA

TESHUVAH – *Forgiving Others*

The one whose forgiveness is sought should forgive with a perfect heart and not be cruel, for such is not the characteristic of an Israelite ... It is customary for the seed of Israel to be slow of anger and easily appeased, and when the sinners ask for forgiveness he should do so wholeheartedly and with a willing soul. Even if he has been grievously wronged, he should not seek vengeance, nor bear a grudge against the other. On the contrary, if the offender does not arouse himself to come unto him to sue for forgiveness, the offended one should present himself to the offender in order that the latter may beg his pardon. If one does not let his enmity pass away, his prayers are not heard on Atonement Day, Heaven forfend, and one who is magnanimous and forgives, has all his own sins forgiven.

KITZUR SHULCHAN ARUCH

Once Rabbi Eleazar ben Rabbi Simeon was coming from Migdal Gedor, from the house of his teacher. He was riding leisurely on his donkey by the riverside, feeling happy and elated because he had studied much Torah. There happened to meet him an exceedingly ugly man who greeted him: "Peace be with you, Sir." But he did not return the greeting, saying instead: "Good for nothing! how ugly you are! Are all your fellow citizens as ugly as you?" The man replied: "I do not know, but go and tell the craftsman who made me, 'How ugly is the vessel which You have made!'" When Rabbi Eleazar realised he had done wrong, he dismounted from the donkey and bowed low before the man, saying: "I submit myself to you, forgive me." The man replied "I will not forgive you until you go to the craftsman who made me and say to Him, 'How ugly is the vessel which You have made.'" He walked behind the man until he reached his native city. When his fellow citizens came out to meet him, greeting him with the words "Peace be with you, O Teacher, O Master.", the man asked: "Whom are you calling Teacher?" They replied: "The man who is walking behind you." At which he exclaimed: "If this man is a teacher, may there not be any more like him in Israel!" When they asked him why, he replied: "He did such and such to me." They said to him: "Nevertheless forgive him, for he is a man greatly learned in Torah." The man replied: "For your sakes I will forgive him, but only on condition that he does not behave in the same way in future." At once Rabbi Eleazar ben Rabbi Simeon entered the Beth Hamidrash and preached on the text: A man should always be gentle as the reed and never unyielding as the cedar. And for this reason the reed merited that it would be made a pen for the writing of the Torah, *Tefillin* and *Mezuzot*.

TA'ANIT

TESHUVAH – *Forgiving Others*

In grief unspeakable, I give you my hand. You are the most pitiable of women; tell your son I forgive him in the name and spirit of the man he murdered; I forgive, even as God may forgive, if before an earthly judge he makes a full confession of his guilt, and before a Heavenly One he repent.
M. RATHENAU, MOTHER OF WALTER, TO HIS ASSASSIN'S MOTHER, 1922

TESHUVAH – *Man and God*

To an earthly king, a man goes full, and returns empty; to God, he goes empty, and returns full.
PESIKTA RABBATI

A king had a son who had gone astray from his father a journey of a hundred days; his friends said to him, "Return to your father"; he said, "I cannot". Then his father sent to say, "Return as far as *you* can, and *I* will come to you the rest of the way". So God says, "Return to Me, and I will return to you".
PESIKTA RABBATI

"He that covers his transgressions shall not prosper, but he who confesses and forsakes them shall obtain mercy". (*Proverbs 28:13*). R. Simeon said: If a man confesses his sin to a human tribunal, he is punished; if he does not, he may be acquitted; but God acts otherwise; if a man does not confess he is punished; if he confesses, he is acquitted.
MIDRASH PSALMS

See how wonderful a thing is repentance! God says, "If you return unto Me, I will return unto you". (*Malachi 3:7*). For however many sins a man may have committed, if he returns to God all are forgiven; He accounts it to him as though he had not sinned (*Ezekiel 18:22*). But if he does not return, God warns him once, twice, thrice. *Then*, if the man returns not, God exacts punishment.
TANCHUMA BERESHIT

Some sins are so great that one can only repent by asserting the same energy against God to force Him to change His mind.
If the Gates of *Teshuvah* are closed, what does one do? Break them down!
Do everything the Baal Habayit (the Master of the house) says – except when He says – "Go!"
q. SHMUEL SPERBER

TESHUVAH — *Man and God*
A Prayer

I am possessed by silent panic,
I am beginning to haggle with God.
I promise him to be a good boy in future
And I whisper to him: "Help me!"

I promise to sin less frequently,
To drink in moderation, to sleep with one girl.
"Please avert the catastrophe,
Hide me behind Your back".

"Beat at the windows like a warm wind,
Grant me an invisible shield!"
I crave His protection, but God
Just isn't that much of a fool.

He remembers in detail
The whole of my backsliding life.
And He thunders in answer: "You, wretch,
Do not blaspheme, do not take My name in vain!"

He probably knows better than my interrogators
That I can never be washed white,
That my promises and actions
Aren't ever likely to agree.

YULI DANIEL (WRITTEN DURING IMPRISONMENT AND INTERROGATION BY THE SOVIET SECRET POLICE)

TESHUVAH — *Preparation*

A tale is told of one who sat in study before the *zaddik* Rabbi Mordecai of Nadvorna, of blessed memory, and before Rosh Hashanah came to obtain permission to be dismissed. That *zaddik* said to him, "Why are you hurrying?"
Said he to him, "I am a Reader, and I must look into the festival prayer book, and put my prayers in order".
Said the *zaddik* to him, "The prayer book is the same as it was last year. But it would be better for you to look into your deeds, and put yourself in order".
S. Y. AGNON

God says to man as he said to Moses: "Put off thy shoes from off thy feet" — put off the habitual which encloses your foot and you will recognize that the place on which you happen to be standing at this

TESHUVAH – *Preparation*

moment is holy ground. For there is no rung of being on which we cannot find the holiness of God everywhere and at all times.

CHASIDIC

Rabbi Nathan David Sidlovtzer, son of Rabbi Yerachmiel, said: "We read: 'As far as the East is from the West, so far hath He removed our transgressions from us' (*Psalms 103:12*). When a man stands facing the east, he needs but a turning about to face west. Likewise a sinner needs but a slight mental turning-about to be far removed from his transgressions".

CHASIDIC

Let the person who wishes to merit *Teshuvah* make it a practice to recite Psalms. There are many barriers to doing *Teshuvah*. One person may not be sufficiently awake and even he who arouses himself faces many barriers, for the gates of *Teshuvah* are shut in the face of many. There are others who do not know how to do it, and pass their days and die, God forbid, without having done *Teshuvah*. But, even if a man is not awake for *Teshuvah*, he will merit the awakening, by reciting of Psalms, and will open all the closed gates and come into the gate of *Teshuvah* that belongs to his particular soul, until he merits a complete *Teshuvah*.

NACHMAN OF BRATZLAV

"Rabbi Eliezer said: Let a man ever first prepare his prayer, and afterward worship" (*Rosh Hashanah 33a*). His dictum is relevant to the blessings of Rosh Hashanah and Yom Kippur, for every man must prepare his prayer in advance so as not to err. This is particularly true of the Reader, who in addition stands in awe of the congregation. Therefore let every man review and study the prayers and liturgical poems to be fluent in the hour of prayer on Rosh Hashanah. Let him teach his children and the members of his household the order of the service and the order of the blessings and the order of the various services, so that he will not need to halt his prayer on Rosh Hashanah to show them the correct order.

MOSES BEN ABRAHAM PREMSLA

TESHUVAH – *The Timing*

R. Eliezer said: "repent one day before your death". His disciples asked him, "Does then one know on what day he will die?" "Then all the more reason that he repent today", he replied, "lest he die tomorrow, and thus his whole life is spent in repentance. And Solomon too said in

TESHUVAH – *The Timing*

his wisdom, Let thy garments be always white, and let not thy head lack ointment". (*Eccles 9:8*)
SHABBAT

"Seek the Lord while He may be found" (*Isaiah 55:6*). This refers to the ten days from Rosh Hashanah to Yom Kippur.
ROSH HASHANAH

Rabbi Mendel Vorker remarked: We read in the Rosh Hashanah Service: "If a man should repent, his repentance would be accepted at once". From this we learn that if merchandise is offered for sale in season it is taken without close examination. But out of season the would-be purchaser examines it closely for minor defects. The Ten Days of Penitence constitute the season for repentance, and therefore a repentance containing minor defects is accepted at that time.
CHASIDIC

The Holy One, blessed be He, said to Israel: Remake yourselves by repentance during the ten days between New Year's Day and the Day of Atonement, and on the Day of Atonement I will hold you guiltless, regarding you as a newly made creature.
PESIKTA RABBATI

It is out of kindness (*chesed*, God's faithful, true love) that the Lord remembers them and reviews their deeds year after year on Rosh Hashanah, that their sins may not grow too numerous, and there may be room for forgiveness, and, being few, He may forgive them. For, if He were not to remember them for a long time, their sins would multiply to such an extent as to doom the world, God forbid. So this revered day assures the world of survival.
SEFER HA CHINUCH

TESHUVAH – *Aids*

The terms of repentance are four in number: 1. the renunciation of sin, 2. remorse, 3. the quest of forgiveness, and 4. the assumption of the obligation not to relapse into sin ...
What device is there for eradicating from men's hearts the thought of lapsing back into sin? My answer is: Thinking up reasons for holding this world in contempt. Let a person remind himself of his condition of impotence, misery, exertion and disillusionment, of his eventual death and the decomposition of the parts of his body, of the vermin and the putrefaction that are destined for him, of the accounting he will have to give for his conduct and the torments to which he will be subjected and

TESHUVAH – *Aids*

whatever appertains to any of these matters. The result of such reflection would be contempt for this world, and once all mundane things are held in contempt by him, his sins would be included in the totality of things to be abstained from and his resolve to abandon them would be intensified ...

To the four conditions of repentance listed previously should be added the following further aids: namely, more extensive prayer, increased charity, and the endeavour to restore men to the path of virtue.

SAADIAH GAON

There are three requisites for repentance: seeing eyes, hearing ears and an understanding heart, ready to return and be healed. Let your eyes see your conduct; let your ears hear words of admonition by our Holy Rabbis; and let your heart understand its eternal purpose. Then you will attain perfect repentance.

NACHMAN OF BRATZLAV

It is narrated that there was once a wicked man who committed all kinds of sins. One day he asked a wise man to teach him the way of repentance in an easy manner, and the latter said to him: "Refrain from telling lies". He went forth joyful and glad of heart, thinking that the wise man permitted him to walk in the stubborness of his heart as before. When he decided to steal, as had been his custom, he reflected: "What am I to do in case somebody asks me; 'Where are you going?' If I tell the truth: 'To steal', I shall be arrested; if I tell a lie, I shall transgress the command of the wise man". In the same manner he reflected on all other sins, and repented with a perfect repentance.

JUDAH BEN ASHER

TESHUVAH – *Hindrances*

The things hindering and preventing repentance are three: ignorance of having committed a sin, excusing oneself, and the love of money and glory. It is clear that every one of these hinders repentance. If a man does not recognize or know that he has sinned, he will never regret doing the thing he does, nor repent, as a sick man cannot be cured as long as he does not feel or know that he is sick, for he will never seek a cure. So if one does not know that he has sinned, he will never repent ... It is also clear from the thing itself that self-excuse prevents repentance. For if a man thinks that excusing himself for his sin will avail him, he will never regret the doing of it, nor confess his sin. Such a one is called a man "who covers his transgressions" ... Covering one's sin means to

TESHUVAH – *Hindrances*

make something else responsible for one's sin ...

Love of money and glory prevents repentance. For if a person repents in order to get some financial benefit or honour, his act is not repentance at all. One must undertake not to return again to folly for the love of God and not for any other motive ...

JOSEPH ALBO

Twenty-four things hinder repentance. Four of these are serious offences ...
1. He who leads the people to sin ...
2. He who diverts another from the good to the evil, such as a seducer or enticer ...
3. He who sees that his son is falling into bad ways and does not stop him...
4. He who says "I will sin and then repent" ...

Five of them block the approaches to repentance ...
1. He who stands aloof from the community ...
2. He who opposes the rulings of the sages ... and thus remains ignorant of the ways of repentance...
3. He who makes a mockery of the divine precepts ...
4. He who insults his teachers ...
5. He who hates rebukes ...

Five of them prevent complete repentance because they affect others who cannot be compensated and forgive ...
1. He who curses the people ...
2. He who shares with a thief ...
3. He who finds lost property and does not announce it, that he may restore it to its owner ...
4. He who takes advantage of the poor, orphans and widows since these people ... are not well known, wander from place to place and cannot be found to be compensated ...
5. He who takes bribes to tamper with justice ...

Five prevent repentance because they seem so trivial that they are not thought of as sins ...
1. He who shares a meal that is insufficient for its owner.
2. He who makes use of a poor man's pledge; since a poor man's pledge happens to be only an axe or a plow, and the user says to himself: "The articles have not depreciated, and I have not robbed him"...
3. He who gazes at women lustfully ...
4. He who elevates himself at the expense of another's degradation ...
5. He who suspects honest men ...

TESHUVAH – *Hindrances*
Five are such that anyone who commits them will always be attached to them, and they are hard to give up ...Gossip; slander; anger; evil thought; keeping bad company.
All these and similar misdeeds do not prevent repentance, even though they hinder it. If a person is sincerely remorseful over them and repents, he is repentant indeed and has a share in the world to come.
MAIMONIDES

TESHUVAH – *The Struggle*

When we examine what our sages have to say on this subject (of sin) we discover that in their opinion the man who longs to sin is worthier and more perfect than the man who has no desire to sin and suffers no pain when he rejects sin. They even went so far as to say that the worthier a man is and the more perfect, the greater will be his desire to sin and his pain in rejecting sin. In this connection they say that the greater the man, the more powerful is his impulse to evil. Not content with this they say that the reward of the man who exercised self-control is in proportion to the amount of pain the effort at self-control causes him. As they say: "According to the amount of pain involved in doing good so is the reward". Even more than this, they positively commanded a man to have the desire to sin and they warned him never to say that he would not commit this sin because of the laws of his nature even if the Torah had not forbidden it. I refer here to the passage: "Rabban Simeon ben Gamaliel said: A man should not say: It is impossible for me to eat milk and meat together, it is impossible for me to wear garments of mixed kinds, it is impossible for me to have a forbidden sexual union. But he should say: It is quite possible for me, but what can I do if my Father in Heaven has commanded me not to do it".
MAIMONIDES

But a great man, in one of the Jewish definitions, has also great faults. It is a very famous saying in Talmud that the greater you are, the greater is your *Yetzer Hara*; your evil desires are stronger. One of the great thinkers of the Hasidic way wrote that it is also right the other way round: the greater the evil in you, you are really greater that way. It is not possible to imagine a man born imbalanced. When you are one of the *Zaddikim*, you have to have also great desires and great temptations. When you are a little fellow, everything about you is little. As one said about it: When you have a precious stone there are two parts to it – the part of preciousness and the material of stone, and you

TESHUVAH – *The Struggle*

cannot part them: the greater is the precious stone, the greater is the stony matter in it. And therefore in a way, it is also right the other way round; when a man finds in himself a very special temptation in a special way, it means that this is his strong point. There he should concentrate and find the solution of his problems, just in the point which is his greatest temptation and his greatest desire, because he is always able to overcome them.
ADIN STEINSALTZ

TESHUVAH – *The Boundaries*

All sins are atoned for by repentance, except such as entail irretrievable harm e.g., corrupting, misleading and misinforming a multitude, ruining the reputation of an innocent person, and keeping misappropriated articles.
SAADIA GAON

We do not ask that our past sins be forgiven in the sense that their effects may be cancelled ... All we can and do ask for is better insight, purer faith, fuller strength.
C. G. MONTEFIORE

You must not think that only such transgressions require repentance as have involved some act, as, for instance, immorality, robbery, theft; but just as one ought to turn from these transgressions, so ought one also to examine the wicked dispositions which he may possess, and to turn from anger, hatred, jealousy, mockery, hunting for wealth and honours, or hunting gluttonously after food etc.; from all these a man ought to turn with repentance. And indeed, these sins are even more serious than those associated with actions inasmuch as when one is sunk in these it is very difficult to extricate oneself from them. Moreover, let not a penitent think that, because of the wrongs and sins of which he has been guilty, he is far removed from the grade attained by the righteous. This is not so; he is as beloved and as pleasing in the eyes of the Creator as if he had never sinned; and indeed his reward will be even greater; for the penitent has tasted of sin, and has nevertheless departed from it, and subdued his inclination. And so have our sages said: Where penitents stand, the wholly righteous cannot stand. This signifies that their position is higher than that of those who have never sinned, for they have had to struggle against their inclinations far more than the others.
MAIMONIDES

TESHUVAH – *True and False*

Who is the penitent man? R. Judah said: The man who when the same opportunity for sin occurs once or twice refrains from sinning. He added: The same woman, the same season, the same place.
YOMA

Our rabbis taught: If a man is guilty of a sin and confesses it but does not change his way, what is he like? Like a man who holds a reptile in his hand, and though he immerse himself in all the waters of the world, it will not help to purify him; but as soon as he throws away the defiling reptile, an immersion in forty *se'ah* of water (the minimum contents of a *Mikveh*, ritual bath) will be accounted to him as a cleansing bath.
TA'ANIT

It is written, "They shall be ashamed who deal treacherously" (*Psalms 25:3*). These are they who fast without repentance.
MIDRASH PSALMS

TESHUVAH – *Israel*

All the prophecy of Israel turns on one simple but extremely difficult idea: namely that *all Israel, living and dead, from Sinai to the present hour, stands in its relation to God as a single immortal individual.* The mass confession stamps that idea at the heart of Yom Kippur ... The covenant that was proclaimed with blasts of the *shofar* (on Mount Sinai) still exists. The immortal individual who entered the covenant still lives. On days of annual judgment and atonement, this individual strikes the balance of his performance under the covenant and confesses his failures to blasts of the *shofar*. And so the compact between God and Israel carries forward into a new year, as it has already done several thousand times.
HERMAN WOUK

When a society pursues false gods and permits injustice to prevail in its midst, the reaction may take the form of internal strife and revolution. A new life will be established upon the ruins of the old, but the new life will face the peril of new corruption, and a new need of cleansing. The striving against the lingering wrongs which pervade every man and group is the mark of the Providence of God, who continues to summon us to remake ourselves and our world in the image of the ideal. This striving is the root of *teshuvah*, or penitence, which will never permit us

TESHUVAH – *Israel*

to remain as we are, which will ever send us in quest for self-improvement.
ABRAHAM ISAAC KOOK

Just as when a garment becomes soiled, it can be made white again, so can Israel return to God after they have sinned, by doing repentance.
EXODUS RABBAH

And so "We" in whose community the individual recognizes his sin, can be nothing less than the congregation of mankind itself. Just as the year, on these days, represents eternity, so Israel represents mankind. Israel is aware of praying "with the sinners". And – no matter what the origin of the obscure phrase may be – this means praying, in the capacity of all of mankind, "with" everyone; for everyone is a sinner.
FRANZ ROSENZWEIG

According to the Old Testament ... forgiveness belongs to God alone ... God *forgives* by calling man into a purpose, a hope beyond that by which he had been content to live. He lures him away from his humanly limited aspirations into an adventure which nothing except the reality of the achievement can justify. He liberates a crowd of slaves, takes them out of a bondage they had learned to take so much for granted that even the desire to break free had become atrophied. He entices them to rebel, against hopeless odds, by reminding them of the imaginary youth of their tribe, of their frustrated youthful desires. He seduces them by vast promises to go where they would never have dared to go. He coaxes them to listen to the commandments that will make men out of slaves and will help them to feel at home in a greater order and harmony. He inspires them to take a land they would not have conquered on their own initiative. *That is His forgiveness.*
WERNER AND LOTTE PELZ

There are so-called leaders versed only in superficialities and outward values. They cannot lead even themselves, and evil impulse prompts them to lead others. They are not so much to be blamed as those who vote for them and support them. These adherents will be called upon eventually to give an accounting for their action.
NACHMAN OF BRATZLAV

A man cannot find redemption until he sees the flaws in his soul, and tries to efface them. Nor can a people be redeemed until it sees the flaws in its soul and tries to efface them. But whether it be a man or a people, whoever shuts out the realization of his flaws is shutting out redemption. We can be redeemed only to the extent to which we see ourselves.
CHASIDIC

TESHUVAH — *The World*

Mankind has the capacity of continual self-renewal, of continual rebirth, of breaking obstructions, of turning ever again to atonement and reconciliation. For the path of history, the good remains mankind's task despite all the bypaths of its errors. As an old saying has it: "A sin may extinguish a commandment, but it cannot extinguish the Torah" — the "light" remains and in its radiance mankind finds its future. As another saying of the Talmud has it, the "Day of Atonement is the day which never ends". When history reaches this day of return, a new epoch begins in it. Then history declares a new covenant with God; life proves itself in history and finds its realization.

LEO BAECK

TESHUVAH AND MESSIAH

"Open to me my sister" (*Song of Songs 5:2*). R. Issi says: God says to the Israelites, Open to Me, My children, the gate of repentance as minutely as the point of a needle, and I will open for you gates wide enough for carriages and wagons to enter through them. R. Levi said: If the Israelites would but repent for one day, they would be redeemed, and the son of David would come straight away, as it says, "Today, if you would hear his voice". (*Psalms 95:7*)

SONG OF SONGS RABBAH

All the calculated ends have already passed (for the coming of the Messiah) and it now depends entirely on repentance and good deeds.

SANHEDRIN

BAALEY TESHUVAH — *Penitents*

R. Elazar ben Durdaya was a great sinner, and much addicted to sexual offences. On one occasion he heard of a beautiful courtesan in a distant land who demanded a purse full of *denarii* as her price. So R. Elazar took a purse full of *denarii*, and crossed seven rivers to the place where she lived ... Afterwards she called out: "You will never be received in repentance!" Then he went away, and sat between two hills, and said, "You hills and mountains, pray for compassion upon me". But they said, "Before we seek for compassion for you, we must seek compassion for ourselves", as it is said, "For the mountains shall depart and the hills be removed". (*Isaiah 54:10*). Then he said, "Earth and heaven, seek for mercy upon me". But they said, "Before we seek mercy for you, we

BAALEY TESHUVAH — *Penitents*

must seek it for ourselves", as it is said, "The moon shall be confounded and the sun ashamed". (*Isaiah 24:23*). Then he said, "You stars and planets, seek for mercy upon me". But they said, "Before we seek mercy for you, we must seek it for ourselves", as it is said, "All the host of heaven shall be dissolved". (*Isaiah 34:4*). Then he said, "The matter depends on no-one but myself!" And he sank his head between his knees, and he cried out and wept until his soul passed out of his body. Then a heavenly voice was heard to say: "R. Elazar ben Durdaya is appointed for the life of the world to come". And Rabbi Judah the Prince wept and said, "There are those who can but attain the world to come in how many years, and there are those who attain it in an hour!" And he said, "It is not enough that the repentant are received into the life to come, but they are even called Rabbis (teachers)." (For the great *Baaley Teshuvah* are pathfinders.)

AVODAH ZARAH

"Against You, You only, have I sinned". (*Psalms 51:4*) (David's psalm of *Teshuvah* after the episode with Bathsheba). With whom may we compare David? With a man who has sustained an injury, and gone to the doctor. The doctor marvels and says to him, "How great is your wound; I am distressed about you". The man replies, "You are distressed about me? Is it not for your advantage that I have been wounded, for the fee is yours?" So David said to God, "For You, You only, have I sinned, so that You may say to transgressors, Why do you not repent? If you receive *me*, then all transgressors will surrender to You, and all will look at me, and I shall be a witness that You receive the penitent".

MIDRASH PSALMS

If a man should come and say that God does not receive the penitent, there is King Manasseh, the son of Hezekiah; let him come and give evidence. For no creature in the world acted so wickedly before Me as he did, yet in the hour of repentance I accepted him; as is borne out by the text, "And he prayed to Him; and He was entreated of him, and heard his supplication, and brought him back to Jerusalem to his kingdom". (*II Chronicles 33:13*)

NUMBERS RABBAH

I returned to the fold of God's lowly creatures, and I acknowledged once more the omnipotence of a supreme Being who presides over the destinies of this world and who in future would direct my own earthly affairs. These had become considerably confused in the period when I was my own providence, and I was glad to hand them over to a

BAALEY TESHUVAH – *Penitents*

heavenly superintendent, as it were, whose omniscience really does enable Him to look after them much better than I could.
HEINRICH HEINE

To have found God is not an end but in itself a beginning.
FRANZ ROSENZWEIG

And I told myself that if I made some other use of my life, if I devoted it to some other study, if later I founded a family without being able to bequeath to my children some ancestral ideal, I should always experience an obscure remorse, the vague feeling of having failed in a duty. And I remembered my dead father, I reproached myself with not having understood that Jewish wisdom of which he talked to me and which lived in him – and with no longer finding, by my own fault, anything in common between Israel's past and my own empty soul.
EDMOND FLEG

O You, my God: all peoples praise You
and avow their humble devotion to You.
So what can it mean to You
if I do so as well, or not.
Who am I to believe
that my prayer is also needed?

When I say "God", I know that I speak of
the unique, eternal, almighty, all-knowing
and inconceivable, of whom I neither can nor
should make any image:
on whom I cannot and should not
lay any claim to fulfil or heed
even my most passionate prayer.

And yet I pray, as all living creatures pray;
and yet I beg for mercies and miracles:
fulfillments.
ARNOLD SCHOENBERG – FROM ONE OF HIS "MODERN PSALMS". HE DIED WHILE SETTING TO MUSIC THE PHRASE "AND YET I PRAY"

TESHUVAH – *Meditations*

A European in the latest mode of dress,
An atheist, an advanced, progressive man.
Yet I have suddenly stopped in my stride,
And fling my arms out – Save and bless!

TESHUVAH — *Meditations*

My suit hangs badly on me, doesn't fit.
My tie is like a rope around my neck,
When the lightning flashes high in heaven,
And the thunder crashes all over it.

I am afraid, therefore I come to You,
Not fawning, not begging, but in despair
I beat both my fists upon Your door,
That You may comfort me and reassure.

I need You, like a mother and a home.
I need You like the bread that comes to me like blood,
Because I am alone,
And don't know what's the good.
MOSHE SHIMMEL

Tonight

An evening at home:
sitting in the house and looking
out of the window.
The wife sits in her chair embroidering
and sewing maybe.
I turn around and look at her: she is just sitting there
not doing anything,
holding idle in her hands
the needle, the scissors, and the cloth,
thinking of our life together, day after day
each with its worries;
how when we have a talk, the important thing always goes unsaid,
and how you never can escape
the habitual and boring routine of daily life;
how every day gone is lost —
it will never come back, never,
and just like today, tomorrow will pass,
and whatever it was you lived for
has defeated you.

She is thinking like this
when hopefully, she looks at you
at the very moment you turn from the window
and look at her too; and in that glance
everything becomes absolutely clear.
So you get up,

TESHUVAH – *Meditations*

go over to her, your own wife,
put a hand gently on her shoulder
and with the other smooth back her hair,
and want to say many loving things
but you can't.
You look out the window again,
the night dark, the stars bright,
and in your heart is peace.

ZISHA LANDAU

It cannot be denied that even our nihilistic time favours us with all sorts of unctuous little maxims, "Be good, be honest, do no evil, think of your fellow-man, don't shirk responsibility, etc.".
To the devil with such tripe! Why should I be good and honest and not do evil and not shirk responsibility? I am only a whirl of some idiotic electrons which paste together a bit of muck, electrons which in a short time will fly apart, not without a stench. There will be no trace of me in the world-process. So it's all the same whether I do evil or good. My feeling of responsibility merely subjects me uncritically to the exploitive purposes of society, be it capitalistic or socialistic. Morality is, in my opinion, only the art of gaining my own ends without becoming a criminal. Well, what do you say? For whom shall I sacrifice myself? For the next generation? For my children? And how do you justify, if I may ask, this queasy, sentimentally humanitarian lie? I am living here and now. The chance will not come again. I will not give it up for anyone.
That business of the future and the children is empty metaphysics, hypocritically dished out by the entire clergy, from the Catholic to the Marxist. I won't be made a fool of! Since nothing has any meaning, the struggle for the satisfaction of my urges is the sole reality.
Thus, in truth, would every ethic be which did not rest in divine affinity...
... Only when we are assured of an eternal perfection do we grow aware of our own imperfection. Only when we are convinced of the eternal continuance of the temporal moment does life appear capable of direction.
The road is clear. It begins here, directly before us. And a very troublesome road it is. It demands work, study, criticism, struggle, solitude, pangs of conscience, decision and renunciation ... But we must hope that the procedure will be of benefit to us. All who are in despair should set forth upon their road. Its goal is the goal of all the world: Joy.

FRANZ WERFEL

TESHUVAH – *First or Last*

Once, we are told, a traveller making his way through a difficult and perilous countryside came to the bank of a river too deep to be forded. Return he could not, nor remain where he was. How, then, was he to come to the other side? Then he bethought himself of the purse which dangled from his girdle, containing in the form of gold pieces all his worldly wealth. In the extremity of his need he began to toss the coins one by one into the river, hoping so to raise a pathway for himself over its bed.

In vain! The bag emptied; the river still could not be crossed.

Finally one gold piece remained. Holding this in his hand, the traveller cast about for some other device. Looking here and there he espied a ferry boat far down the river which in his frenzy he had failed to notice earlier. Regretting that he had wasted his treasure to no purpose, yet fortunate in that one coin was left to him for passage money, he hastened to the boat, gave the gold piece to the ferryman and crossed to the other side, so saving his life and going on his way.

Bahya Ibn Pakuda ... was trying to say that penitence ought to be man's first expenditure, but that it proves too often his last – the sole remaining device available to him when all else has been spent ...

For the wise and the prudent it is the first coin in the purse – that disbursment of the spirit which makes possible the negotiating of life's most dreadful passages – which enables men to go on their way safe and rejoicing.

But for the foolish, the insensitive, the reckless, the undiscerning, it is the last coin in the purse, the one which – when every resource has been exhausted, when man is left with only his need and desperation – purchases a secure crossing to fresh possibilities and new hopes.

MILTON STEINBERG

TEFILAH – *Prayer*

Prayer is not a stratagem for occasional use, a refuge to resort to now and then. It is rather like an established residence for the innermost self. All things have a home, the bird has a nest, the fox has a hole, the bee has a hive. A soul without prayer is a soul without a home. Weary, sobbing, the soul, after running through a world festered with aimlessness, falsehoods and absurdities, seeks a moment in which to gather up its scattered life, in which to divest itself of enforced pretensions and camouflage, in which to simplify complexities, in which to call for help without being a coward. Such a home is prayer.

TEFILAH – *Prayer*

Continuity, permanence, intimacy, authenticity, earnestness are its attributes. For the soul, home is where prayer is ...
How marvellous is my home. I enter as a suppliant and emerge as a witness; I enter as a stranger and emerge as next of kin. I may enter spiritually shapeless, inwardly disfigured, and emerge wholly changed. It is in moments of prayer that my image is forged, that my striving is fashioned. To understand the world I must have my home. It is difficult to perceive luminosity anywhere if there is no light in my own home. It is in the light of prayer's radiance that I find my way even in the dark. It is prayer that illumines my way. As my prayers, so is my understanding.
ABRAHAM JOSHUA HESCHEL

One is asked: how do I learn to pray? There is really only one answer: pray!
Pray other people's prayers. You will appropriate them to yourself by using them and pouring your own personality into them. Do not wait until you "feel like" praying, or until you know how to pray. You never will. This is really a case of "we shall do and then hear". And even if we could occasionally speak without having to use the thoughts and words of others, how shabby and sentimentally self-indulgent such worship invariably turns out to be! "In a sense, our liturgy is a higher form of silence ... The spirit of Israel speaks, the self is silent".
STEVEN S. SCHWARZSCHILD

... But there can be a real "service of the heart" only when that service is truly a *service*, that is, a service rendered to God by the man who feels *obligated* to render such a service ...
Rabbi Eliezer Berkovits has described that relationship of voluntary to obligatory prayer ... "When a man, overwhelmed by the impact of a specific experience, seeks the nearness of God or bursts forth in halleluyah or bows down in gratitude, it is prayer but not service of God yet; it is a human response to a potent stimulus. But when he prays without the stimulus of a specific occasion, acknowledging that man is always dependent on God, that independently of all personal experiences God is always to be praised and to be thanked, then – and only then – is prayer divine service of the heart.
JAKOB J. PETUCHOWSKI

God must also be thought capable of saying "No!" Perhaps this is indeed the major difference between engaging in magic and engaging in prayer. Magic, by definition, *must* work. If it does not yield results, then, in the view of the practitioner of magic, something must have

TEFILAH – *Prayer*

gone wrong with the performance of the magical rite; and he will repeat the rite in a more careful and meticulous manner. Prayer, on the other hand, is addressed to a God who has a will and a mind of His own. God cannot be manipulated by man. He can only be *addressed*. He may, or may not grant a specific request. But there is no mechanism of man's devising which would compel Him to do so. In addressing God, man knows that a "No" can be as much of an "answer" as a "Yes". Moreover, a divine "answer" is already implicit in man's very capacity to pray. Here we have in mind man's capacity to invest the words of prayer with real personal meaning and significance, and not just the ability to *read* the words printed in the prayer book. My very ability to pray shows me that I am "in tune" with the divine will, that I am assured of divine help in my striving for the realization of the goals formulated in my prayers. Perhaps that is the true meaning of the Prophetic utterance: "And it shall come to pass that, before they call, I will answer, and while they are yet speaking, I will hear". (*Isaiah 65:24*).
JAKOB J. PETUCHOWSKI

Reb Arele (R. Aharon Rote) returns to the same theme several times: inability to pray and abstinence from prayer are marks of the truly pious person. "It was furthermore written in the name of the Besht, may his memory be for a blessing, that if a man gets into some kind of trouble, Heaven forfend and may it not happen, then it is the best thing not to pray at all at that time about his troubles. Let him merely very much strengthen his heart in God with trust in his Lord, for then 'Israel will be saved by God'" ...

Here, clearly, was a man who knew, who must have experienced, what real anguish is. He says: if you can still pray, you are not really in trouble yet, for you still have the strength to pray. You are in real trouble when you cannot pray any more. But this lowest point in human existence, precisely because it is the lowest, is also closest to salvation. You cannot help yourself any more; now God must, and will, help. The birth-pangs of redemption must precede redemption.
STEVEN S. SCHWARZSCHILD

PRAYER

If one asks the meaning of praying three times a day, there is a simple explantion. For it is fitting for a man to dedicate himself to God in worship by means of his body, his soul and his wealth, as it says: "Love the Lord your God with all your heart, and all your soul, and all your might."

PRAYER

"With all your heart" refers to your body, since our sages explained that "all your heart" refers to the two impulses, to good and to evil, and that the impulse to evil is a drive within the body of man.

"With all your soul" — even if He takes your soul from you.

"With all your might" — even if He takes your "might", your wealth, from you.

Since the sleep of the morning is the most refreshing for man, as the body is functioning but the mind is at rest, and since man really desires to continue this morning sleep, it is right for him to overcome himself and rise from his sleep and pray, and thus man dedicates his body to God by overcoming his body's desire.

Afternoon prayer comes in the main part of the day when man is most intensely engaged in his work — so if he takes time off to turn to God in prayer, he dedicates his wealth to God.

And when it is evening and a man is tired from his daily tasks with all their anxieties, and his soul seeks its rest, nevertheless at this time, too, he should dedicate his soul to God and pray.

Thus by the three daily prayers man dedicates to God all three things which he possesses — body, wealth and soul.

MAHARAL OF PRAGUE

Lord, I am weary, yet I dare not pray
That Thou wilt ease me of my load.
At Thy command I bear it all the day,
And Thou hast traced my road.

Lord, I am fearful of the shades of night,
That darkening o'er my path descend,
Yet vain it were to pray for lengthening light,
That I my task may end.

Lord, I am troubled, yet I will not plead
With Thee for days of happiness,
While all around I see my brethren's need,
Their anguish and distress.

Lord, be it so! I will not ask of Thee
To give me rest from toil and care,
Or length of days, but this alone shall be
My heart's unceasing prayer.

Lord, grant to me, nor yet to me alone,
But unto all on earth who dwell,
Faith that Thy love, through ways to us unknown
Doth order all things well.

PRAYER

Lord, grant us faith, then, though we work and weep,
Thy peace will guard us on our way,
And we shall lay us down in peace, and sleep
When comes the close of day.
ALICE LUCAS

ZEDAKAH – *Charity*

R. Johanan said: So long as the Temple was in existence, the altar used to atone for Israel, but now a man's table atones for him. (The poor may be fed from his table, or he may have them as guests).
BERACHOT

In the Temple there was a Chamber of Secret Charity. God-fearing people used to deposit their contributions in it secretly, and the poor who were descended from well-to-do families were supported from it in secret.
MISHNAH SHEKALIM

Often a man makes his heart to do a charitable act, but the impulse to evil within him says: "Why practise charity and reduce your possessions? Rather than give to strangers, give to your children". But the good impulse prompts him to do charity.
EXODUS RABBAH

Said the Leover: "If someone comes to you for assistance and you say to him: 'God will help you', you become a disloyal servant of God. It is for you to understand that God has sent you to aid the needy, and not to refer him back to God".
CHASIDIC

What you save from frivolity, add to your charity.
ELIJAH BEN RAPHAEL

A community which has no synagogue and no shelter for the poor, must first provide for the poor.
SEFER CHASIDIM

By benevolence a man rises to a height where he meets God. Therefore do a good deed before you begin your prayers.
AHAI GAON

The community leaders of Medziboz, the Besht's home town, decided to abolish the custom of placing charity plates at the entrance of the synagogue on the day before Yom Kippur. The noise caused by this almsgiving interfered with the decorum of the Services.

ZEDAKAH – *Charity*

The Besht opposed the decision saying: "The sound of audible alms-giving dispels all unholy thoughts".
CHASIDIC

He who sustains God's creatures is as though he had created them.
TANCHUMA

Though you may have given already, give yet again even a hundred times, for it says, "Give, surely give ..." (*Deut 15:10*)
SIFRE

It is taught in the name of R. Joshua: The poor man does more for the rich man than the rich man for the poor man.
RUTH RABBAH

In the future world man will be asked, "What was your occupation?" If he reply, "I fed the hungry", then they reply, "This is the gate of the Lord; he who feeds the hungry, let him enter" (*Psalms 118:20*). So with giving drink to the thirsty, clothing the naked, with those who look after orphans, and with those, generally, who do deeds of loving kindness. All these are gates of the Lord, and those who do such deeds shall enter within them.
MIDRASH PSALMS

One can always find warm hearts who in a glow of emotion would like to make the whole world happy but who have never attempted the sober experiment of bringing a real blessing to a single human being. It is easy to revel enthusiastically in one's love of man, but it is more difficult to do good to someone solely because he is a human being. When we are approached by a human being demanding his right, we cannot replace definite ethical action by mere vague good will. How often has the mere love of one's neighbour been able to compromise and hold its peace!
All love of man, if it is not to be mere unfruitful sentimentality, must have its roots in the ethical and social will, in the inner recognition of man, in the vital respect of his right – in what is meant by *Zedakah*. That is primary and fundamental, alone making a clear and irrefutable demand which admits of no evasion.
LEO BAECK

The verse states "Happy is he that considers the poor" (*Psalms 41:2*). Said Rabbi Jonah: Note that it is not written "happy is he that gives to the poor" but "that considers the poor". Consider well how to help him without offending his dignity.
LEVITICUS RABBAH

ZEDAKAH – *Charity*

After the evening service of Yom Kippur, Rabbi Joseph Dov Ber Soloveitchik of Brisk observed that a wealthy member of his congregation remained in the synagogue to recite psalms. The sage said to him reproachfully:

"Every soldier in an army is assigned to a division — artillery, cavalry, or infantry. Naturally, he has no authority to change from one division to another. If he does change without permission of the proper authorities, he is considered a deserter and he has to face a court-martial.

"Every Jew is a soldier in the army of the Lord and is given an assignment which he cannot change without authorization. The recital of psalms is the assignment given to the poor for repentance on the Day of Atonement. However, to you, as one blessed with riches, has been assigned the duty of giving charity to fulfil your responsibility for repentance. If you don't want to be court-martialled by the Celestial Court, you had better fulfil your own assignment".

CHASIDIC

He who pities the poor shall himself receive compassion from the Holy One, blessed be He. Let man further reflect that as there is a wheel of fortune revolving in this world, perchance some day either he himself, or his son, or his son's son, may be brought down to the same lowly state. Nor let it enter his mind to say: "How can I give to the poor and thus lessen my possessions?" For man must know that he is not the master of what he has, but only the guardian, to carry out the will of Him who entrusted these things to his keeping.

Whosoever withholds alms from the needy thereby withdraws himself from the lustre of the *Shechinah* (the presence of God) and the light of the Torah.

Let man therefore be exceedingly diligent in the right bestowal of charity.

JACOB BEN ASHER

ATONEMENT

The translation of *kapper*, "to make atonement", does not render the original meaning of the word. But there is another translation which makes this clearer: to cover. The sin is covered. That is atonement. An action cannot be undone, just as yesterday cannot be recalled. But something else is possible. The action can be atoned. Whether this be in the fire of judgment or in the compassion of forgiveness, in both cases it concerns the mystery of God, "who in His goodness reneweth the

ATONEMENT

creation every day continually". The sin is covered, it no longer cries to Heaven, it does not pollute the land. Now life is possible. The sons begin in a renewed creation, unencumbered by the sins of the fathers. That is the miracle of the compassionate God.
IGNAZ MAYBAUM

ATONEMENT – *Intimations*

"It has only been in the last two centuries that the majority of people in civilized countries have claimed the privilege of being individuals. Formerly they were slave, peasant, labourer, even artisan, but not person. It is clear that this revolution, a triumph for justice in many ways ... has also introduced new kinds of grief and misery, and so far, on the broadest scale, it has not been altogether a success ... For a historian, of great interest, but for one aware of the suffering it is appalling. Hearts that get no real wage, souls that find no nourishment. Falsehoods, unlimited. Desire, unlimited. Possibility, unlimited ... The idea of the uniqueness of the soul. An excellent idea. A true idea. But in these forms? In these poor forms. Dear God! With hair, with clothes, with drugs and cosmetics, with genitalia, with round trips through evil, monstrosity, and orgy, with even God approached through obscenities? How terrified the soul must be in this vehemence.
SAUL BELLOW

"Where is the dwelling of God?"
This is the question with which the Rabbi of Kotzk surprised a number of learned men who happened to be visiting him.
They laughed at him: "What a thing to ask! Is not the whole world full of His glory?"
Then he answered his own question:
"God dwells wherever man lets Him in".
This is the ultimate purpose: to let God in. But we can let Him in only where we really stand, where we live, where we live a true life. If we maintain holy intercourse with the little world entrusted to us, if we help the holy spiritual substance to accomplish itself in that section of Creation in which we are living, then we are establishing, in this our place, a dwelling for the Divine Presence.
MARTIN BUBER

HIGH HOLYDAYS

Three books are opened in Heaven on the New Year: one for recording

HIGH HOLYDAYS

the thoroughly wicked, one for the thoroughly righteous, and one for the intermediate category. The thoroughly righteous are at once written for reward, and the thoroughly wicked for punishment. But the fate of the intermediate category, which includes most of us, if not all, is suspended from the New Year to the Day of Atonement. If we deserve well, we are then written down in the Book of Life; if not, we are written down in the book of punishment.
ROSH HASHANAH

The High Holydays form part of the reality of what it means to exist as a Jew ... In this annual "return", liturgy and social forces, the faith of a people and the feeling of being a people, the God of Israel and the potential godliness of the children of Israel, are closely interwoven. That "one band" which we are exhorted to form, to "perform the will of heaven", is on this single occasion given partial fulfillment ... *Teshuvah*, "return" is a vital concept underwriting the corrigibility of human nature, and the hope that reconciliation of man with man and man with the Eternal, is possible. The *Al Chet*, "for the sins", is an acknowledgment that we have fallen short in our personal relationships, and assumes that we possess the freedom to correct them. The *Malchuth Shamayim*, the kingship of God, affirms that despite our sense of finitude, anxiety and guilt, we can hope for transcendence.
MICHAEL GOULSTON

The New Year and the Day of Atonement put before us the thought of peace, inner peace before God, and peace with our neighbour, and make therefore our striving for peace for mankind a religious obligation. The need for *Teshuvah*, for return to a religious conception of life, is so incumbent upon us that the great assembly of Israel on the threshold of a new year must not be religious pretence but, in all sincerity, a new attempt. The Jew knows that in order to be a good man he must "return" to be a good Jew, he must return to the teachings of the prophets and sages of his people. We must not only confess within and without our community peace as a religious aim, but commit ourselves to it.

There should be peace foremost in the Camp of all Israel, despite existing religous differences. The real proof for living peace is not the peace among the like-minded but among those who differ. Peace and tolerance are words that in our time flow easily from our lips. New Year and Atonement underline the Jewish conception of *enacting* them. We are asked not only to pray for peace, to think of it, but still more to live it. The hand outstretched to our neighbour for the sake of peace is a significant Jewish symbol of our High Festivals.
W. VAN DER ZYL

ROSH HASHANAH — *The Birthday of the World*

In the beginning God created the heavens and the earth.
GENESIS 1:1

Lord, our Lord, how glorious is Your name
in all the earth!
When I look up at Your heavens, the work of Your hands,
the moon and the stars You set in place,
what is man that You should remember him
or the son of man that You should care for him.
You have made him little less than divine
and crowned him with glory and splendour.
You gave him power over the works of Your hands,
You put all things beneath his foot.
Sheep and cattle, all of them,
also the beasts of the field,
the birds of the air, and the fish of the sea,
who make their way through the oceans.
Lord, our Lord, how glorious is Your name
in all the earth!
(FROM PSALM 8)

Lord, how many are Your works,
with wisdom You made them all
the earth is full of Your creatures.
This vast expanse of ocean!
There go swarms of creeping creatures
all forms of life, great and small!
There go the ships,
the sea monsters You formed to play with —
All of them depend on You
to give them food when it is needed.
You give it to them — they gather it.
You open Your hand — they eat their fill.
You hide Your face — they vanish.
You take back Your spirit — they die,
and return to their dust.
You give breath — they are created,
and You renew the face of the earth.
(FROM PSALM 104)

ROSH HASHANAH — *The Birthday of the World*

This day the world was called into being; this day all the creatures of the universe stand in judgment before You.
MUSAPH SERVICE FOR ROSH HASHANAH

Avinu Malkenu, it is He who, on the birthday of His world, comforts His children and makes them brothers and sisters, all the loving fathers and mothers and their threatened and rescued children. As it always does, here, too, the thing most individual depends on the universal: the world is reborn in the individual human being.
ERNST SIMON

"Love your neighbour as yourself; I am the Lord" (*Lev 19:18*). There is a Chasidic interpretation of the last words of this verse: "I am the Lord." — "You think that I am far away from you, but in your love for your neighbour you will find Me; not in his love for you but in your love for him." He who loves brings God and the world together.
The meaning of this teaching is: You *yourself* must begin. Existence will remain meaningless for you if you yourself do not penetrate into it with active love and if you do not in this way discover its meaning for yourself. Everything is waiting to be hallowed by you; it is waiting to be disclosed and to be realized by you. For the sake of this your beginning, God created the world.
MARTIN BUBER

"The people which shall be created shall praise the Lord" (*Psalms 102:18*). Is there another people to be created in the future? The Rabbis say that "people" means "the generations which have made themselves guilty by their evil deeds, and they come and repent, and pray before God on New Year and the Day of Atonement, and if they make their deeds new, then God creates them, as it were, into new creatures."
MIDRASH PSALMS

ROSH HASHANAH — *Meditations*

I love calm lives
That pass like quiet Sabbaths
Across ordinary weekdays.
These intricate souls
That are coiled round life like an endless tale,
They seem to walk on tiptoe
Close against the wall,
Listening to a hidden singer on the other side.

ROSH HASHANAH – *Meditations*

They seem to see a guiding hand on the other side.
Through generations and epochs
They smile at each other from the distance,
Like little flames in the midst of a black night.
I love them, those calm calm lives.
Y. DOBRUSHIN (DIED IN A SIBERIAN PRISON CAMP)

I've Lost

I think I have lost something on the way.
What it is I do not know.
Shall I turn back? It is so far off now.
Yet it is a pity to let it go.

I have lost something, but do not know what.
Is it anything of worth?
I shall let it lie – for the day is short,
And vast is the earth.

Already the shadows fall from the trees.
Long falls my shadow.
My heart is unquiet. It cries – turn back.
My loss torments me so.

So I stand still in the midst of the road,
Tormented, doubt-tossed.
I have lost something, but do not know what.
But I know that I've lost.
ABRAHAM REISEN

The House of God

The house of God will never close to them that yearn,
Nor will the wicks die out that in the branches turn;
And all the pathways to God's house will be converging,
In quest of nests the migrant pigeons will come surging.

And when at close of crimson nights and frenzied days,
You'll writhe in darkness and will struggle in a maze
Of demons' toils, with ashes strewn upon your head,
And lead-shot blood, and quicksand for your feet to tread
The silent house of God will stand in silent glade.
It will not chide, or blame, or scoff, will not upbraid.
The door will be wide open and the light will burn,
And none will beckon you and none repel with stern
Rebuke. For upon the threshold Love will wait to bless
And heal your bleeding wound and soothe your sore distress ...
YEHOASH

ROSH HASHANAH – *Meditations*

There is no area of our existence in which fate has not cut its furrows deeply into our lives. We are not speaking of the disappearance of external prestige, nor of the separation from habitual and much loved activities which forced many to begin a new existence. Rather we feel that we, as no generation in many an age, confront our fate nakedly. The ground on which our feet stand is shaken, and for most of us it is still uncertain in which part of the earth we might find a new foothold. Tragedies of love and death, the deepest encounters of man with his fate, all this we experience in its starkest and most variegated forms, and many nearly collapse under its over-powering force. For what a hard trial it is for each individual when ties between parents and children, brothers and sisters and friends, are torn asunder, when a loved one now lives far away and thereby has disappeared irrevocably as if death had taken him. How are we to bear it, to see death so unexpectedly near in our own physical life? Death, as we hear from Palestine every day, may come more quickly and suddenly than we had ever suspected.

No wonder that many a one is seized by the fear that life is playing an incomprehensible game with him, and in his confusion he himself begins to think little of his life. But beyond all this is the worst: the inner anxiety which has grasped many of our people today, that fear of tomorrow which makes it impossible to bear the today. Like mill stones the same cares and thoughts turn again and again in his mind, shattering his nerves, destroying his powers. It seems as if the worst curse which the Bible expresses is to be fulfilled: "In the morning you shall say: 'if only it were evening', and in the evening: 'if only it were morning!'" ...

We stand naked before our fate, but thereby we are not only without the many things which formerly assisted us, but we are freed also of the ballast of prejudice, of the habits and conventions which narrowed our field of vision. We want to face reality, but we also do not want to give ourselves over to a fatalism which releases us from all obligations. We want to love our life because of, not despite, the fact that it has revealed itself to us in all its elemental power.

With such sentiments we prepare ourselves for the High Holydays of our year. We will miss this time many a familiar face that we saw in past years in the Temple. Many a place which was used by the same family for three or four generations will be empty. The portals of many synagogues in small communities will remain closed and in many places people already wonder whether a *minyan* can still be brought together. But during these days, all Jews hear the sound of the *Shofar.* From the

ROSH HASHANAH – *Meditations*

synagogues of this land, from the places of worship of all the lands of the earth which might become new homes for Jewish people, even from the rooms of transatlantic steamers, the prayer rises with strength and devotion rarely heard before, that we might be inscribed in the Book of Life for a good year.

DER MORGEN (ONE OF THE LAST ARTICLES PUBLISHED IN A JEWISH MAGAZINE IN GERMANY SHORTLY BEFORE THE SECOND WORLD WAR)

SHALIACH TZIBBUR – *"The Representative of the Congregation", the Reader.*

The Baal Shem Tov came to a certain city before Rosh Hashanah. He asked the inhabitants who was their Reader during the Service on the Solemn Days. The reply was, "The Rabbi of the city". Thereupon the Besht asked, "What is his custom during his prayer?" They replied, "He weds all the Confessions of Yom Kippur to joyful melodies". The Besht sent for the Rabbi and asked him, "Why do you recite the Confession so joyfully?" The Rabbi replied, "When a royal slave removes unsightly things from his master's courtyard, he is happy because he has done it out of love for him. Similarly do I rejoice when I remove objectionable things from my heart, for thereby I give pleasure to the King of Kings". Then the Besht replied, "May my portion be with you".
CHASIDIC

Nor is any Reader appointed who has enemies in the congregation. Rabbi Meir ben Isaac Katzenellenbogen wrote in his Responsa, "And if the congregation desire him for their Reader, he is obligated to remove the hatred from his heart, and to say explicitly that he will include his enemy in his prayer, the same as every other man". Now the same was the custom of the ancients; when a man could sense a feeling of ill will against him in the heart of the Reader, he would compel the Reader to say that he would include him in his prayer.
S. Y. AGNON

The devout and saintly men of Yemen refuse to be Readers, for the Reader takes the place of the High Priest, and the prayers of the community must pass through him. Therefore, if his thoughts should be distracted from his prayer even for a moment, or if he should slip over a single word, his prayer would not be heard on high, and the prayer of those who send him to be their emissary would not be accepted. It follows that he bears the iniquity of all the folk, and the Holy One, blessed be He, can call him to account at once. Hence, whosoever undertakes to be a Reader is honoured by the people as though he were

SHALIACH TZIBBUR — *"The Representative of the Congregation", the Reader.*

offering himself as a communal sacrifice.
S. Y. AGNON

It is fitting that the Reader know how to awaken the heart of the folk to devotion, with a joyful melody where joy and enthusiasm are needed, and with a tearful melody where weeping is needed for confession and Teshuvah. But let the Reader not show himself vain because of his melodies.
S. Y. AGNON

KITTEL

On Rosh Hashanah and Yom Kippur, Jews do not appear depressed and in dark clothes, but joyous, dressed in festive white, as a mark of a cheerful and confident spirit.
YERUSHALMI ROSH HASHANAH

Death is the ultimate, the boundary of creation ... Man is utterly alone on the day of his death, when he is clothed in his shroud, and in the prayers of these days he is also alone. They too set him, lonely and naked, straight before the throne of God. In time to come, God will judge him solely by his own deeds and the thoughts of his own heart. God will not ask about those around him and what they have done to help him or to corrupt him. He will be judged solely according to what he himself has done and thought. On the Days of Awe, too, he confronts the eyes of his judge in utter loneliness, as if he were dead in the midst of life, a member of the community of man which, like himself, has placed itself beyond the grave in the very fullness of living ... And God lifts up his countenance to this united and lonely pleading of men in their shrouds, men beyond the grave, of a community of souls ...
FRANZ ROSENZWEIG

1.
A man should remember, from time to time,
That he is occupied with death,
That he is taken a little further
On a journey every day
Though he thinks he is at rest,
Like a ship's passenger lounging on deck,
Being carried on by the wings of the wind.

KITTEL

2.
I was stirred to visit the resting place
Of my parents and all my true friends.
I questioned them, but they neither heard
Nor answered me. Have even, I asked,
My own mother and father betrayed me?
Without speaking they called to me
And showed me my own place beside them.
3.
There are graves remaining from long ago
In which men sleep out eternity.
There is neither envy nor hatred,
Love nor malice there, and looking
Over them I could not separate
Who was slave and who was master.
MOSES IBN EZRA

The shroud should always be kept clean and ready.
MAASEY BOOK

Shrouds are made without pockets.
YIDDISH PROVERB

FASTING

Four main reasons are given for the command to fast on *Yom Kippur*.
Fasting as a penance. The most obvious reason for fasting on *Yom Kippur* is that by this means we show contrition for the wrong we have done and the good we have failed to do ... Most people feel the need to give of themselves, to make some sacrifice, in order to demonstrate that their protestations of remorse mean something and are more than lip service. Self-affliction ... in moderation is an act affirming a man's sincerity. The man who fasts for his sins is saying in so many words, I do not want to be let off lightly; I deserve to be punished.
Fasting as self-discipline. Self-indulgence and lack of self-control frequently lead to sin. It is natural that repentance be preceded by an attempt at self-discipline. Disciplining oneself is never easy but all religious teachers have insisted on its value ... The traditional Jewish character ideal is for a person to be harsh with himself but indulgent towards others. Fasting on *Yom Kippur* serves as a potent reminder for the need of the self-discipline which leads to self-improvement.
Fasting as a means of focussing the mind on the spiritual. It has been

FASTING

noted frequently that Judaism frankly recognizes the bodily instincts and the need for their legitimate gratification. And yet ... religion seeks to encourage and foster the spiritual side of man's life. By fasting on *Yom Kippur* the needs of the body are left unattended for twenty four hours and the Jew gives all his concentration to the things of the spirit. Scripture says that "no man shall be in the tent of meeting" (*Lev 16:17*) when the High Priest enters to make atonement there on *Yom Kippur*. This is taken by the *Midrash* to mean that at that awful hour the High Priest was "no man", his body became ethereal like that of the angels. This is what happens to every Jew who observes the day as it should be observed.

Fasting as a means of awakening compassion. By knowing what it means to go hungry, albeit for a day, our hearts are moved for those who suffer. By fasting we are moved to think of the needs of others and to alleviate their suffering.

LOUIS JACOBS

The Elders of the congregation addressed the worshippers with words of admonition: Brethren, it is not said of the men of Nineveh, "And God saw their sackcloth and their fasting", but "God saw their works, that they turned from their evil way". (*Jonah 3:10*)

MISHNAH TAANIT

Contrition for sins is a greater penance than fasting.

NACHMAN OF BRATZLAV

"Why have we fasted, yet You do not see?
Why have we afflicted our souls, yet You pay no heed?"
Because it is for strife and contention that you fast,
so as to strike with a fist of wickedness.
You do not fast this day
to make your voices heard on high.
Is such the fast that I have chosen?
The day for a man to afflict his soul?
Is it to bow down his head as a bullrush,
and spread sackcloth and ashes beneath him?
Will you call this a fast,
and a day acceptable to the Lord?
Is not this the fast I have chosen?
To loose the fetters of wickedness,
to undo the bands of the yoke,
to let the oppressed go free
to break every yoke?

FASTING

Is it not sharing your food with the hungry
and bringing the homeless into your home,
clothing the destitute when you meet them
and not evading your duty to your own flesh and blood.
ISAIAH 58:3-7

And the changes of the liturgical year are marked out for the Jew by smell and taste, by the aromas of the kitchen. Through the most basic senses, he feels the changing moods of the spirit. Theologies alter and beliefs may die, but smells always remain in his memory, calling him back to his own childhood and to the childhood of his people. Whatever prayers he may forget, the gastronomic cycle always remains. Passover is the bread of poverty, with tears of salt water and the horseradish of bitterness. Ruth is cream and cheesecake, and the New Year is the sweetness of apples and honey. Esther comes with poppy seed, and the Maccabees with nuts. The delightful litany only halts to mark the destruction of the past, or days which commemorate the sins of the present. On these tragic and sad days there is a total fast, and the kitchen, the heart and soul of the Jewish home, misses a beat, and darkness covers this little world.
LIONEL BLUE

CONFESSION

The first step towards repentance, which is the most essential and at the same time the most difficult is confession, or rather "the admission to oneself" that one has sinned. It is not God who needs an avowal or confession from us, for He knows us through and through; in fact, much better than we know ourselves. But we ourselves stand very much in need of honest and unreserved confession; it is to our own selves that we must admit that we have done wrong.
SAMSON RAPHAEL HIRSCH

Why was the Confession couched in the plural form so that we say, "We have sinned", and not "I have sinned"? This is because all Israel is one body, and each individual Jew is a limb of this body. And when his fellowman commits a sin, it is as if he himself had committed it. Therefore, even if he has not committed any particular sin he must confess it, for when his fellow sins, it is as if he himself had transgressed.
ISAAC LURIA

The sinner who craves forgiveness confesses; which is reasonable, if only one knew how adequately to confess. And so there are the ingenious

CONFESSION

lists arranged in alphabetical order. Since for people with the fear of God in them even a list from A to Z seems abridged, the sentences are doubled for each letter; two for A and two for B and two for C; and when the alphabet gives out, there are still categories to refer to, such as "For the sins for which we owe a burnt-offering ... for which we owe a sin-offering ... for which we deserve the punishment of ..." ...
"Yom Kippur makes atonement for transgressions committed in man's relations with the Omnipresent. But Yom Kippur does not make atonement for transgressions in men's relationships with one another, until the transgressor has appeased his fellow". In other words, confession brings relief when there is genuine reform. Yom Kippur has little tolerance for humbug.
JUDAH GOLDIN

As to the kinds of sins confessed, be it noted that they are nearly everyone of them transgressions against *our fellowmen*. A large number are evil thoughts, failings, and sins against our *own higher nature*. Both the Shorter and Longer Confessions deal exclusively with ethical lapses. There are some remarkable omissions. Thus, among the very many moral offences enumerated, no mention is made of brutal assaults, bestial cruelty, or murder. To the creators of these Confessions, as well as to the People who in all the centuries sought reconciliation with their Maker through them, these crimes of violence were in their eyes something so unspeakably horrible, that it appeared inconceivable how any Jew could be guilty of them.
J. H. HERTZ

The Berditschever chanced to pass the night at a wayside inn. He heard a thief in the next room relating to his comrade the story of his work the night before.
"What a holy people is Israel!" exclaimed the Rabbi. "It is still a long time to *Selichoth*, yet the man has already begun to confess his sins".
CHASIDIC

Question: Why on the Day of Atonement, is the confession of sins given in alphabetical order?
Answer: If it were otherwise we should not know when to stop beating our breast. For there is no end to sin, and no end to the awareness of sin, but there *is* an end to the alphabet.
CHASIDIC

"I make confession before Thee ..."
Lord God be not wroth with me,
Look down and see what has become

CONFESSION
Of Thy child far away from home.
Many lands and troubles everywhere.
I no longer remember the prayer.

"I make confession before Thee ..."
The memory of it has escaped me,
All because of a clean bed,
A night's rest and a piece of bread.
I have suffered everywhere.
And have forgotten the prayer.

"I make confession before Thee ..."
By devious paths and erringly
I wandered, Lord God, seeking Thee.
I am young and full of perplexity,
And strangers have been misleading me.
Lord God I make confession before Thee.
MARK SCHWEID

CONFESSION – *The Problem*

The breast-beating (during the prayer *Al Chet*) was carried out with varying degrees of intensity; my father did it quietly, but an ultra-orthodox old man at the corner of the very top row, who had a special little reading-stand of the swivelling kind for his prayer books and commentaries in addition to the ordinary ledge, made a tremendous to-do with his beatings and groanings. Some people on the other hand – they must have been rather *link* – didn't beat at all. There was nothing hypocritical, in the ordinary sense of the word, about this breast-beating or about the actual confession, and when I used the words "meaningless formulae" I didn't intend to imply anything of the kind; what I meant was that the words and the gestures accompanying them, and the emotion involved, had no living relation with any individual, as an individual, at the Bayswater Synagogue in Chichester Place in the year nineteen hundred and so and so, nor was remotely intended to have, but was a kind of traditional performance, and at that level sincere; for by taking part in this performance Jews were simply manifesting as Jews, and nothing could have been sincerer than that. When I complained to my parents that I had never "committed a sin before thee" by "the taking of bribes", or "in business", or "by usury or interest", or by "wanton looks", I was told that this had nothing to do with the matter: the reference was not to me or my parents or Mr.

CONFESSION – *The Problem*

Isaacs or Mr. Cohen, but to the whole House of Israel collectively. This maddened me; House of Israel or no House of Israel, how could I, Victor Gollancz of two hundred and fifty-six Elgin Avenue, Maida Vale, include myself in the "we" who had been wicked in business when I wasn't in business at all! ...

I find, on looking through the prayer-book to refresh my memory, that I was in fact personally guilty, as no doubt was almost everybody else in greater or lesser degree, of many of the sins for which we made confession in the *Al Chet*. Hardening of the heart; wronging our neighbour, sinful meditation; unclean lips; denying and lying; "the stretched forth neck of pride", effrontery; envy; levity; stiff-neckedness; "confusion of mind" (certainly, but how could I help it?); even perhaps, on second thoughts, "wanton looks" – not only do I now know that most if not all of these things were ingredients in my character, as many of them still are, but I was painfully aware of it then. But you will utterly fail to understand what I have been getting at unless you realise that, just as confessing a thing didn't and in some cases quite obviously couldn't imply that you'd done it, so confessing what in fact you *had* done didn't necessarily imply that you were aware of having done it; nor again did confessing what you couldn't help knowing you'd done necessarily imply that you sincerely repented of it and would try not to do it again ...

Do not, I beg of you, misunderstand me. I am not suggesting, God forbid, that repentance was impossible, or never occurred, on the Day of Atonement: knowledge of such matters is with the Almighty and the person concerned. I am suggesting this: It was a desire, deep in the Jewish consciousness, to heal the breach with God that led to the establishment of *Kippur*. But out of the very intensity of this desire, out of an anxiety to make the effort complete and leave nothing unprovided for, there developed a machinery of observances, uniform for everyone; and this machinery had ended by so occupying the field as almost to preclude that free intercourse between the individual and God without which restoration, reconciliation, at-one-ment is forever impossible. The qualification "almost" is important; first because there is a last remnant of spiritual spontaneity in almost everyone, and secondly because there are some rare types so spiritually strong that they can turn the most unpromising material to good account. There must have been people in my parents' circle, however few, who found the Day of Atonement just the occasion that they spiritually needed.
VICTOR GOLLANCZ

MALCHUYOT – *Kingship of God*

"When God had created the world ... He produced on the second day the angels with their natural inclination to do good, and an absolute inability to commit sin. On the following days He created the beasts with their exclusively animal desires. But He was pleased with neither of these extremes. 'If the angels follow My will,' said God, 'it is only on account of their inability to act in the opposite direction. I shall, therefore, create man, who will be a combination of both angel and beast, so that he will be able to follow either the good or the evil inclination.'" ...

In short it is not slaves, heaven-born though they may be, that can make the kingdom glorious. God wants to reign over free agents, and it is their obedience which He desires to obtain. Man becomes thus the centre of creation, for he is the only object in which the kingship could come into full expression. Hence it is, as it would seem, that on the sixth day, after God had finished all His work, including man, that God became king over the world.
SOLOMON SCHECHTER

If, then, the kingdom of God was thus originally intended to be in the midst of men and for men at large (as represented by Adam), if its first preachers were, like Abraham, ex-heathens, who addressed themselves to heathens, if, again, the essence of their preaching was righteousness and justice, and if, lastly, the kingdom does not mean a hierarchy, but any form of government conducted on the principles of righteousness, holiness, justice and charitableness, then we may safely maintain that the kingdom of God, as taught by Judaism in one of its aspects, is universal in its aims.
Hence the universal tone generally prevalent in all the kingship prayers.
SOLOMON SCHECHTER

The sovereignty of man is dependant upon the sovereignty of God; that a man should view every act which he performs as the fulfillment of the wish of the kingdom of Heaven. This is the meaning of the oft-repeated Talmudic injunction that man should act "for the sake of Heaven", and take upon himself "the yoke of the Kingdom of Heaven".
SAMUEL BELKIN

The kingdom of God is not a kingdom above the world or opposed to it or even side by side with it ... It is not a future of miracle for which man can only wait, but a future of commandment which always has its present and ever demands a beginning and decision from man ... Man

MALCHUYOT – *Kingship of God*

must choose this kingdom. It is the kingdom of piety into which man enters through the moral service of God, through the conviction that the divine will is not something foreign to him or parallel to his life but the fulfillment of his days. He who knows and acknowledges God through never-ending good deeds is on the road to the kingdom of God ...
LEO BAECK

The "Kingdom" of God is not that which is to be established "at the end of time" or "beyond history" or in another worldly existence. The "Kingdom" of God is already here now. God's sovereign will established and maintains the laws of heaven and earth (*Jer 33:25*) and by His will the destiny of men and nations is decreed. It is therefore not the "Kingdom" of God which man must affirm but His *Kingship* ... For us, the *Mitzvot* are the means whereby we declare that God "not only reigns in the world, but that He also governs our personal lives".
MAX ARZT

God's kingdom is ... more than a promise. Obscured and broken though it be, latent rather than overt, it is also an ever-present actuality. Everything in the world subserving goodness is of its dominion. Everyone ministering to the right is, whether knowingly or not, its citizen.

Touch Judaism where you will and you will come upon this concept of the Kingdom, this dream of a perfected world peopled by regenerated men ...

When then the Kingdom has come at last, when the final evil has been broken and the remotest good achieved, the glory of that moment will belong to all the men past and present who have dreamed of it and striven toward it.

But the deeper glory will belong to Him who through the ages has spurred mankind, often against its will, to the greater good and beyond that to the greatest.

In that hour men, departed and living alike, will have abundant reason to chant together the litany of the Psalmist:

"Not unto us, O Lord, not unto us, but unto Thy name give glory."
MILTON STEINBERG

THE SHOFAR

The law to blow the *Shofar* on Rosh Hashanah has a profound meaning. It says, "Awake, you sleepers, and ponder on your deeds; remember your Creator and go back to Him in penitence. Be not of those who

THE SHOFAR

miss reality in their pursuit of shadows and waste their years in seeking after vain things which cannot profit or help. Look well to your souls and consider your acts; forsake each of you his evil ways and thoughts, and return to God, so that He may have mercy upon you.

MAIMONIDES

There are ten reasons why the Creator, blessed be He, commanded us to sound the *Shofar* on Rosh Hashanah.

1. Because this day is the beginning of creation, on which the Holy One, blessed be He, created the world and reigned over it ...
2. Because the day of New Year is the first of the ten days of repentance, the *Shofar* is sounded on it to announce to us as one warns and says: "Whoever wants to repent — let him repent; and if he does not, let him reproach himself". Thus do the kings: first they warn the people of their decrees; then if one violates a decree after the warning, his excuse is not accepted.
3. To remind us of Mount Sinai ... and that we should accept for ourselves the covenant that our ancestors accepted for themselves ...
4. To remind us of the words of the prophets that were compared to the sound of the *Shofar*, as it is said: "Then whoever hears the sound of the horn, and accepts not the warning, if the sword come and take him away, his blood shall be upon his own head ... whereas if he had taken warning, he would have delivered his soul". (*Ezekiel 33:4-5*)
5. To remind us of the destruction of the Temple, and the sound of the battle-cries of the enemies ... When we hear the sound of the *Shofar*, we will ask God to rebuild the Temple.
6. To remind us of the binding of Isaac who offered his life to Heaven. We also should offer our lives for the sanctification of His Name, and thus we will be remembered for good.
7. When we will hear the blowing of the *Shofar*, we will be fearful, and we will tremble, and we will humble ourselves before the Creator, for that is the nature of the *Shofar* — it causes fear and trembling.
8. To recall the day of the great judgment and to be fearful of it.
9. To remind us of the ingathering of the scattered ones of Israel, that we ardently desire.
10. To remind us of the resurrection of the dead and the belief in it.

SAADIAH GAON

For the *Shofar* of Rosh Hashanah, whose purpose it is to rouse the purely divine in man, no artificially constructed piece of work may be sounded. It must be an instrument in its natural form (naturally hollow), with life given to it by the breath of man, speaking to the

THE SHOFAR

spirit of man. For you cannot attain to God by artificial means or by artifice. And no sound which charms the senses, but which does not appeal to man's better self, can raise you to God — indeed, you might surrender yourself again to your low, base way of living.
SAMSON RAPHAEL HIRSCH

Rabbi Levi Yitzhak of Berditzchev was interrogating a number of candidates for the blowing of the *Shofar* on Rosh Hashanah. He asked each one: "What will be your thoughts while you blow the *Shofar*?" He was dissatisfied by the variety of pious sentiments voiced by the candidates until one of them said:
"Rabbi, I'm a simple, poor Jew. I have four daughters who have long ago reached the marriage age but I am unable to provide dowries for them. When I will blow the *Shofar*, I will bear my daughters in mind. I will think: 'Merciful One! I am fulfilling the commandments You have ordained. Give ear to the *Shofar* sound beseeching You to fulfil your obligation of providing dowries for my daughters'".
The straightforward, sincere honesty of this Jew appealed to Levi Yitzhak and he engaged him to sound the *Shofar*.
CHASIDIC

The three notes *tekiah*, *shevarim*, *teruah* have received the attention of the symbolists. One view sees the three notes of weeping as different degrees of contrition, another view sees the *tekiah* as the optimistic note of confidence and hope that weeping will be turned to joy. Others interpret the three sounds as hesitation in approaching the King leading to increasing confidence as the suppliant is made welcome. Others again teach that the three notes correspond to three types of men. The firm, unwavering *tekiah* represents the good man, whose soul is undivided. The trembling *teruah* represents the wicked, full of remorse and regret, his soul torn in his unsuccessful struggle against evil. The *shevarim*, the partly broken notes, represent the average man, neither wholly good nor bad. who tries sincerely to make his life more complete.
LOUIS JACOBS

A quarrelsome, cantankerous man may not be chosen to blow the *Shofar*, because of the principle of Rabbinic law, "A prosecutor cannot act as a defender". One who is accusing and complaining all the year cannot now act as Israel's defense this day.
SEFER CHASIDIM

TEN DAYS — *Meditations*

O my soul, set your heart toward the highway, the way by which you have walked; for all was made of dust, and indeed all shall return to dust. Everything that was created and fashioned has an end and a goal to return to the ground from which it was taken. Life and death are brothers that dwell together; they cling together and cannot be drawn apart. They are joined together by the two ends of a frail bridge over which all created beings pass: life is the way in and death is the way out; life builds and death demolishes; life sows and death reaps; life plants and death uproots; life unites and death separates; life links together and death scatters. Therefore know and see that the cup will pass over to you as well, and you shall soon go from the lodging place that is on the way, when time and chance befall you, and you return to your eternal home. On that day you shall delight in your work, and take your reward for the labour in which you toiled, whether it be good or bad ...

O my soul, prepare provisions in abundance, prepare not little while you are yet alive and your hand has strength, because the journey is too great for you. And do not say: "Tomorrow will I make provision", for the day has declined and you know not what the next day may bring. Know also that yesterday will never return and that whatever you have done then is weighed, numbered and counted. And do not say: "Tomorrow I will do it", for the day of death is hidden from all the living ... Seek the Lord your Maker with all your might and strength. Seek righteousness, seek meekness ... Now arise, go and pray to the Lord, and take up a song to your God. Praise the Lord, for it is good to sing praises to our God; for it is pleasant and praise is fitting.

BACHYA IBN PAKUDA

No lighted Sabbath candles
On your table come.
The drab and dreary week-days
Never leave your home.

Your door has no *mezuzah* —
No angels enter through.
You sing no praises to your wife,
"A woman of virtue".

Your children grow like strangers,
For our faith they have no thought,
They never pray to God, for you
Such things have never taught.

TEN DAYS – *Meditations*

The Seder night you have not kept
For many a year,
Your heart is no longer stirred
By the *Kol Nidre* prayer.

And therefore when you come to die,
No angel will mourn,
And there will be no *Kaddish* said
By your first or later born.
ISRAEL JACOB SCHWARTZ

Give me of Your light and of Your grace,
Wipe from me all trace of wickedness,
My lips are eager for the ray of Your joyousness
That You conceal and mask from me;
Blind mystery hides Your face from me.
My memory and name have waned among my nearest;
And none ask for me.

Estranged from everything and all,
I seek but You, but You I seek.
I wait, I wait,
I lie and weep with longing for You.
Enter my door that is ajar,
My forlorn home,
Be with me.

Ah, good Lord, You are so far away,
Move not farther still from me.
I. I. SEGAL

Man enters the world and knows not why,
and rejoices and knows not the reason,
and lives and knows not how long.
In his childhood he walks in his own stubbornness,
and when the spirit of lust begins in its season
to stir him up to gather power and wealth,
then he journeys from his place to ride in ships and tread the deserts,
and to carry his life to dens of lions walking among wild beasts.
And when he imagines his glory is great
and mighty the spoil in his hand
quietly steals the spoiler upon him, his eyes open and there is nothing.
At every moment he is destined to troubles that pass and return,
and at every hour evils, at every moment chances and every day terrors ...

TEN DAYS – *Meditations*

The man whom these things befall,
when shall he find a time for repentance
to scour away the rust of his perversion?
For the day is short and the work is great,
and the task-masters urgent, hurrying and scurrying,
and time laughs at him and the Master of the House is pressing.
Therefore I beseech You, my God,
remember the distresses that come upon man,
and if I have done evil may You, Yourself, do me good at my end
and not repay measure for measure, to man whose sins are measureless
and whose death is a joyless departure.
SOLOMON IBN GABIROL

Who is like You, revealing the deeps,
Fearful in praises, doing wonders?

The Creator who discovers all from nothing,
Is revealed to the heart, but not to the eye;
Therefore ask not how nor where —
For He fills heaven and earth.

Remove lust from the midst of you;
You will find your God within your bosom,
Walking gently in your heart —
He that brings low and that lifts up.

And see the way of the soul's secret;
Search it out and refresh yourself.
He will make you wise, and you will find freedom,
For you are a captive and the world is a prison.

Make knowledge the envoy between yourself and Him;
Annul your will and do His will;
And know that wheresoever you hide yourself, there is His eye,
And nothing is too hard for Him.

He was the Living while there was yet no dust of the world;
And He is the Maker and He the Bearer;
And man is counted as a fading flower —
Soon to fade, as fades a leaf.
JUDAH HALEVI

Servants of time — the slaves of slaves are they;
The Lord's servant, he alone is free.
Therefore when each man seeks his portion,
"The Lord is my portion", says my soul.
JUDAH HALEVI

TEN DAYS — *Meditations*

Lord, do Thou guide me on my pilgrim way,
Then shall I be at peace, whate'er betide me;
The morn is dark, the clouds hang low and grey,
Lord, do Thou guide me.

Let not the mists of sin from Thee divide me,
But pierce their gloom with mercy's golden ray,
Then shall I know that Thou in love hast tried me.

O'er rugged paths be Thou my staff and stay,
Beneath Thy wings from storm and tempest hide me,
Through life to death, through death to heavenly day
Lord, do Thou guide me.
ALICE LUCAS

KOL NIDRE — *Meaning*

There is and there can be no faith in man where the sense of holiness has gone. You can have faith only in one who keeps his word, to whom his written guarantee is holy, even when it is against his own interests. That is why the conception "holiness" held such a central position in the world of religious ideas, and why all the social protection and social welfare institutions were with the ancient peoples associated with their holy places. The sanctuary was a place of refuge for all who were oppressed, the holy days and the festivals (the Sabbath and the seventh year) had important social functions; to break your word, your bond, your oath, your vow, your covenant made in the name of God, was with the Jews the supreme crime. Without this idea of holiness it is impossible to have respect for human life and the human personality.
A. MENES

Rabbi Moshe Mordecai Epstein (1863-1933), head of the Yeshivah of Slabodka, offered an interesting reinterpretation of the concluding words of the *Kol Nidre*. He suggested that we should regard them as a confession of our lack of moral constancy. The self-righteousness and smugness which stand in the way of our spiritual growth need to be dispelled by a confession, in utter humility, that so often the vows we make are no vows, our resolves no resolves, and our oaths no oaths. When accompanied by such a meditation, the recital of *Kol Nidre* prepares us for the soul-cleansing experience of the Yom Kippur day.
MAX ARZT

KOL NIDRE – *Meditations*

In this hour all Israel stands before God, the judge and the forgiver. In His presence let us all examine our ways, our deeds, and what we have failed to do.
Where we transgressed, let us openly confess: "We have sinned!" and, determined to return to God, let us pray: "Forgive us".
We stand before our God.
With the same fervour with which we confess our sins, the sins of the individual and the sins of the community, do we, in indignation and abhorrence, express our contempt for the lies concerning us and the defamation of our religion and its testimonies.
We have trust in our faith and in our future.
Who made known to the world the mystery of the Eternal, the One God?
Who imparted to the world the comprehension of purity of conduct and purity of family life?
Who taught the world respect for man, created in the image of God?
Who spoke of the commandment of righteousness, of social justice?
In all this were seen manifest the spirit of the prophets, the divine revelation to the Jewish people. It grew out of our Judaism and is still growing. By these facts we repel the insults flung at us.
We stand before our God. On Him we rely. From Him issues the truth and the glory of our history, our fortitude amidst all change of fortune, our endurance in distress.
Our history is a history of nobility of soul, of human dignity. It is history we have recourse to when attack and grievous wrong are directed against us, when affliction and calamity befall us.
God has led our fathers from generation to generation. He will guide us and our children through these days.
We stand before our God, strengthened by His commandment that we fulfil. We bow to Him and stand erect before men. We worship Him and remain firm in all vicissitudes. Humbly we trust in Him and our path lies clear before us; we see our future.
All Israel stands before her God in this hour. In our prayers, in our hope, in our confession, we are one with all Jews on earth. We look upon each other and know who we are; we look up to our God and know what shall abide.
"Behold, He that keepeth Israel doth neither slumber nor sleep" (*Psalms 121:4*).

KOL NIDRE – *Meditations*

"May He who makes peace in His heights bring peace upon us and upon all Israel".

LEO BAECK (PRAYER RECITED ON THE EVE OF KOL NIDRE IN GERMANY 1935, FOLLOWING WHICH HE WAS ARRESTED)

Take away my shame,
Lift my anxiety,
Absolve me of my sin
And enable me to pray before Thee
With gladness of heart,
To pursue Thy commandments and Thy Torah
In the joy of holiness.
Grant me
To bring happiness to all Thy children,
To exalt and ennoble Thy faithful,
To spread goodness and mercy
And blessing in the world.
Humble the arrogant
Who have tried to pervert me with falsehood
While I sought my happiness in serving Thee.
Save me from weakness
And from faltering
And from every evil trait,
Illumine my eyes
With the light of Thy deliverance.
Help Thy people,
Imbue the heart of Thy people with reverence
And with awe before Thy majesty.
Strengthen them with Thy love,
Guide them to walk in the path of Thy righteousness,
Kindle in their hearts
The light of the holiness of this Day of Holiness
And bring them to possess the inheritance
Thou hast set for them,
Speedily, speedily, in our time, soon.
Amen.

ABRAHAM ISAAC KOOK

Before I was born Your love enveloped me.
You turned nothing into substance, and created me.
Who etched out my frame? Who poured
Me into a vessel and moulded me?

KOL NIDRE — *Meditations*

Who breathed a spirit into me? Who opened
the womb of Sheol and extracted me?
Who has guided me from youth-time until now?
Taught me knowledge, and cared wondrously for me?
Truly, I am nothing but clay within Your hand.
It is You, not I, who have really fashioned me.
I confess my sin to You, and do not say
That a serpent intrigued, and tempted me.
How can I conceal from You my faults, since
Before I was born Your love enveloped me?
SOLOMON IBN GABIROL

Night and day, and somberly I dress
In dark attire and consciously confess
According to the printed words, for sins
Suddenly remembered, all the ins
And outs, tricks, deals, and necessary lies
Regretted now, but then quite right and wise.

The benches in the *shul* are new. So this
Is what my ticket bought last year; I miss
My easy chair, this wood is hard, and I
Have changed my mind, refuse to stand and lie
About repentance. No regrets at all.
Why chain myself to a dead branch, I fall
In estimation of my neighbours who
Would have me be a liberated Jew
Ridiculing mediaeval ways
Keep up with them in each swift modern craze
To dedicate our souls to modern taste
To concentrate our minds on endless waste.

"Mediaeval" must be too new a term
For deeper, longer, truer, something firm
Within me used the word "waste". Despite years
Assimilating lack of faith, the fears
My father felt of God, their will to know
That vanity and greed were far below
The final aim of life will help me, too,
Atone, and be a Jew, and be a Jew.
HOWARD HARRISON

THE DAY OF ATONEMENT — *Meaning*

The Holy One, blessed be He, said to Israel: Remake yourselves by repentance during the ten days between New Year's Day and the Day of Atonement, and on the Day of Atonement I will hold you guiltless, regarding you as a newly made creature.
PESIKTA RABBATI

If a man said, "I will sin and repent, and sin again and repent", he will be given no chance to repent. If he said, "I will sin and the Day of Atonement will effect atonement", then the Day of Atonement effects no atonement. For transgressions that are between man and God the Day of Atonement effects atonement, but for transgressions that are between a man and his fellow the Day of Atonement effects atonement only if he has appeased his fellow.
YOMA

Yom Kippur is one of the most universal of our holydays. This means that in essence, not in form, it concerns all men. "There is not a righteous man upon earth, who doeth good and sinneth not", said Ecclesiastes. That is to say, the problems of sin and forgiveness are human problems. All religions have to solve them in their own way. The Jewish Day of Atonement is unique in the manner of its observance, and its appeal finds a response in every truly Jewish heart. We are taught in our religious life to balance emotion with reason. Both have their place. On Yom Kippur both the appeal and the response are far more to the heart than to the mind. We Jews are, as Moses called our forefathers, let us confess it, a stiff-necked people. On the Day of Atonement, our arrogance, our self-will, our sense of independence, our worldliness drop from us "like a garment". In the solemn thought of the great poet Gabirol, each Israelite is pictured as standing before God on this day: "I am bare and destitute of good works and Thy righteousness alone is my covering." Thus does the Jew face himself and his God on Yom Kippur with humility, yet with confidence and hope.
VIVIAN G. SIMMONS

THE DAY OF ATONEMENT — *Meditations*

Lord, I Want to Return

Lord, I want to return to Your word,
Lord, I want to pour out my wine,

THE DAY OF ATONEMENT – *Meditations*

Lord, I want to go, to go to You,
Lord, I do not know what should be done,
I am alone.
I am alone in empty air,
In terror of myself, alone at heart,
All my gay balloons are wan and slack,
All my wisdom chaff and spray,
I am poor. Come back! ....
KARL WOLFSKEHL

Lord, Do Not Turn From Me

Lord, do not turn from me,
I faltered from the fold,
Am I upon Your way?
In haste to slip Your hold?
I shift and drift and stray.
Who tells me that I am
And am upon Your way?
KARL WOLFSKEHL

Day of Atonement

Oh God of mercy, of repentance,
Your people stands with sob and moan,
And prays forgiveness for its sins,
And beats its breast. But I alone
My lips are shut and will not pray.
My eye is hard, as hard as stone.
Yet God, me too forgive, I am Your child,
And in my heart I also sob and moan.
ABRAHAM VIEVIORKA

I find it is Yom Kippur,
                          and here I am
Down by the river
                  in late afternoon.
There is a poem
               I have read
In several versions,
                  about the Jewish writer
Who doesn't fast, who
                  doesn't go to synagogue

THE DAY OF ATONEMENT – *Meditations*
On Yom Kippur,
                the day of atonement,
And here is my construction
                      of that poem.

Here am I,
        on the embankment
Staring at the river,
              while the lights
Are coming up,
              signifying darkness, the end of the fast,
Though it's not over yet,
              and the congregations,
Are still gathered
            in the synagogues,
Praying, *slach lonu, m'chal lonu,*
                  forgive us, pardon us,
We have sinned,
          we deserve punishment,
We are like clay
          in the hands of the great Potter,
Who has shaped us all,
            even, you could say, me
Here by the river,
            watching the water
And the rubbish
          drifting on the water,
Imagining what is
            swaying in under the bridges,
Is something of exile,
              formless but perceptible,
Bringing in the names
            of pious cities,
Vilna and Minsk and Vitebsk
                  (my own ancestral names)
And vanished communities,
            behind curtains
Of forgetfulness,
          and ordinary human change,
Praying communities
            on Yom Kippur and other days

THE DAY OF ATONEMENT – *Meditations*

Clinging to and turning from,
                        that which I cling to
And turn from,
           if you like the covenant
That keeps me fasting,
                   but not in synagogue
To-day, Yom Kippur.
                 I go into the gardens
Sit down on a bench,
               read my newspaper,
And wait
      for the first star.

ARTHUR JACOBS

MARTYROLOGY

At the end of the afternoon prayers, there is a passage describing in rather cruel and realistic colours, the torments of the ten martyrs, teachers and leaders of Israel at the time of Hadrian. The angels of Heaven, seeing these horrible tortures, cry out bitterly, "Is such the Torah, and are such its rewards?!" And they receive an answer that is no answer: "And a voice ... answered from the heavens: Such is My decree, accept it!" And the worshippers in the synagogue, after hearing this terrible tale, respond, saying, "God the King, who sits in the seat of mercy!"

If Jews praying in the synagogue were fully to grasp what they are saying here as part of the afternoon services of the Day of Atonement, they would be shaken to the core. The description of the torments is awful enough, but even more so is the dialogue between God and the angels. And after these two terrifying passages, comes the response and the congregation of worshippers, as though they were a chorus in ancient tragedy answers in spite of everything: the seat of mercy! This is the classical Jewish certainty, a faith that has come to us from our father Abraham, from the Binding of Isaac.

The one who prays knows – with the knowledge of experience – that beyond the visible dimensions of this world there is a hidden dimension of our existence in which something of the significance of a man's being is revealed to him, revealed to a greater or lesser degreee, in keeping with the strength of the communion. It is a matter of experience, and experience, as is well known, is not debatable ...

Learn, with the whole of your ability to learn, all that you can of

MARTYROLOGY

"devekuth" (communion with God)! Learn in the place where you are, within the circumstances, complexities, joys and sorrows in which you find yourself, learn *through* these involvements, to understand — with heart, not head — the meanings that emanate from them. No one can take this task from you. No one else can do this work for you. Faith speaks to you and me, and it relies on the experience of those greater than us. The world is not blind, is not meaningless. Redemption awaits us just behind the curtain. It is not given to an individual man to draw this curtain aside and bring about the redemption. But he isn't compelled to sit and wait, without doing anything. It is given to him to be a *partner* in the act of redemption. By a man's opening in himself the inner sources through which flows and rises the light of redemption for the individual, in keeping with his ability to receive it, the Kingdom of Heaven grows and increases in the world. And the active hope of many individuals will bring the total redemption nearer. That is the hope of Israel.

S. H. BERGMAN

What was most tragic in this Jewish tragedy of the twentieth century was that those who suffered it knew that it was pointless and that they were guiltless. Their forefathers and ancestors of mediaeval times had at least known what they suffered for; for their belief, for their law. They had still possessed a talisman of the soul which today's generation had long since lost, the inviolable faith in their God ... Only now, since they were swept up like dirt in the streets and heaped together, the bankers from their Berlin palaces and sextons from the synagogues of orthodox congregations, the philosophy professors from Paris and Rumanian cabbies, the undertaker's helpers and Nobel prize winners, the concert singers and hired mourners, the authors and distillers, the haves and the have-nots, the great and the small, the devout and the liberals, the usurers and the sages, the Zionists and the assimilated, the Ashkenazim and the Sephardim, the just and the unjust, besides which the confused horde who thought that they had long since eluded the curse, the baptized and semi-Jews — only now, for the first time in hundreds of years, the Jews were forced into a community of interest to which they had long ceased to be sensitive, the ever-recurring — since Egypt — community of expulsion. But why this fate for them and always for them alone? What was the reason, the sense, the aim of this senseless persecution? They were driven out of lands but without a land to go to. They were expelled but not told where they might be accepted. They were held blameful but denied means of expiation. And thus, with smarting eyes, they stared at each other on their flight: Why I? Why

MARTYROLOGY

you? How do you and I who do not know each other, who speak different languages, whose thinking takes different forms and who have nothing in common, happen to be here together? Why any of us? And none could answer.
STEFAN ZWEIG

Our road is not one of cowardice. It is the road of the spirit. It is the strategy of continual retreat, of tragic endurance. The enemy exhausts himself chasing us from land to land and is lost in the forest of our history. The web of our spirit is stronger than barbed wire. Our land will not be conquered. No one can steal heaven. They will not destroy our people. What do we need to be a people? The Jews are a *minyan*, and where there is a *minyan* there is the Jewish people.
CHAIM LIEBERMAN

That's the difficulty in these times: ideals, dreams and cherished hopes rise within us, only to meet the horrible truth and be shattered.
It's really a wonder that I haven't dropped all my ideals, because they seem so absurd and impossible to carry out. Yet I keep them, because in spite of everything I still believe that people are really good at heart. I simply can't build up my hopes on a foundation consisting of confusion, misery, and death. I see the world gradually being turned into a wilderness, I hear the ever-approaching thunder, which will destroy us too, I can feel the sufferings of millions and yet, if I look up into the heavens, I think that it will all come right, that this cruelty too will end, and that peace and tranquillity will return again.
In the meantime, I must uphold my ideals, for perhaps the time will come when I shall be able to carry them out.
ANNE FRANK (DIARY JULY 15, 1944)

Jews don't plant the grain.
Jews sell things in a store.
Jews get bald when young.
Jews steal more.

Jews are a tricky crew.
They make poor soldiers too.
Ivan fights a battle;
Abie hears money rattle.

Ever since my childhood,
I've heard the same old news.
I'll grow old but I won't escape it:
The shouting, "Jews!" "Jews!"

MARTYROLOGY

I never sold a thing.
I never stole a thing.
But I carry my pedigree
Like a plague that curses me.

Somehow a bullet missed me,
So they talk (This is not a lie):
"Jews were never killed! See!
All of them come back alive!"

But we Jews have a certain luck.
When evil came, it wore no hood,
And used no false flag when it struck,
Made no pretensions to be good.

Throughout this solemn, silent land,
With time not ripe yet for debate,
We found the wall where we must stand,
The point for levering our fate.

ANONYMOUS RUSSIAN POET

Every evening when my seven-year-old son returns from school, I lock the door to my room and begin to air out his mind which they packed full all day long with Five Year Plans for producing tractors, with defamation of God's Name, with debunking of Judaism and humanity — "Recite the daily verse!" — "Bubby!" he shouts in his sweet melodious voice. "There is no God. You can't even see Him in the microscope". I stare at my child and tremble. He appears to me as a magician who keeps pulling out of his mouth all sorts of coloured handkerchiefs and threads.
I open the old worn Bible. His two plummed eyes are open. He listens. I read from the book of *Genesis*. — "Daddy, how lovely it sounds! — Daddy, is it true? — Daddy, who wrote this marvelous book?" Weeks pass. Each evening, another chapter. Jacob's dream, and my son searches for the ladder of God. Joseph's confession, and my heart flutters on. My little son is engulfed by another world, a province of exalted figures, noble impressions, divine thoughts.
But tomorrow he returns to school, and they'll drill those same blasphemies against the Bible and all its gifts. There, scores of them; I am but one. Who will triumph?

ELISHA RODIN (IN A SIBERIAN LABOUR CAMP)

MARTYROLOGY

For our Jewish life devastated,
I pray to You, oh God!
I weep for Mother Vilna,
For Kolomeo and for Brod.

For Warsaw, Kovno, Kalish, Lemberg,
For towns both great and small
That have fallen to the conqueror,
Or still await their fall.

For every dirty Jewish alley,
I am grief-stricken, desolate.
For every drinking-bar and pawnshop,
And for our false measure and weight.

For every Jewish brothel
That stood in a non-Jewish town,
For all that once was ours,
And now has been burnt down.

They are all so lovely, things Jewish!
Our impoverished life rebuild!
And speak the word that is wanting,
That our anguish may be stilled!

ZISHA LANDAU

It Had To Be

We were not worthy to die for You — a holy death,
As witnesses to Your covenant, for Your holy breath.
We were not worthy, we forgot we must wait and wait,
In gaudy gardens we revelled and danced.
And our laughter — from drunken lips it spawned
In every hour — until Your hour dawned!
Lord, until You rose and came close,
Took in Your hands the lightning of Your wrath,
In both Your hands — Ah! Your wrath is a scourge,
And still Your wrath elects, and we emerge
Reborn in the well of vengeance of the Lord,
An iron army, Your own once more.
Now death may be a grant from You again,
Now mow and weigh and winnow Your grain.

KARL WOLFSKEHL

MARTYROLOGY

More pathetic than the fasts themselves (of local communities in the middle ages) were the martyrologies and elegies recited in the synagogue. These sad records are scattered over the mediaeval history of the Jews with an all too lavish hand; persecution and cruelty, even unto death, knew no bounds of time or place. But the recital of these elegies generated heroic endurance in the worshipper's mind rather than vindictiveness; they were a call to courage and devotion, and if they appealed to God for revenge, the revenge was idealized almost as much as were the sorrows that demanded it.

Thy son is once more sold,
Redeem him, bring Thou relief!
In mercy say again: My son,
I know, I know thy grief.

ISRAEL ABRAHAMS

Some people profess to see the Holocaust as an ineluctable stage in Jewish history — the labour pains of national rebirth, so to speak, or the price of redemption. One hears this kind of interpretation from extreme nationalists as well as from certain extremely religious Jews. This I shall never be able to understand. I shall never be able to believe in a Guardian of Israel who claims the lives of a million children as the price of national revival.

Did those million die a martyr's death for the Sanctification of the Name? A great many of them were killed without ever having had this feeling. Did they, then, die in vain, more of the innumerable victims of man's bestiality throughout history?

Was the Holocaust nothing but an act of degradation which can only arouse searing pain and endless horror? Or was there, perhaps, beyond the unbelievable indignity, some terrible majesty and magnificence to the Holocaust? By this I do not mean only the manifestations of heroism and courage in the Warsaw ghetto revolt and the struggle of the Jewish partisans.

Rather do I mean that in the vast perspective of history, the Holocaust assumes the grandiose dimensions of a confrontation between the two diametrically opposed world views about which Nietsche spoke: between morality and paganism; between the sanctity of life and the cult of warfare; between the equality of all men and the supremacy of the select few; between the search for truth and the display of vitality; between the quest for justice and the discharge of instinctive impulses; between the vision of a genuine society of equals and the prospect of a society of masters lording it over slaves.

J. L. TALMON

MARTYROLOGY

From tomorrow on I shall be sad,
From tomorrow on.
Not today. Today I will be glad.
And every day, no matter how bitter it may be,
I shall say:
From tomorrow on I shall be sad,
Not today.
(WRITTEN BY AN UNKNOWN CHILD IN A NAZI DEATH CAMP)

When the people of the camp, by the thousands, were brought into the forecourt of the chambers of destruction in Treblinka, they turned to the rabbi and said: "Our rabbi, what do you say now?" The holy rabbi answered them quietly: "Hearken, my brothers and my sisters, O people of God! We may not criticize God's deeds. If it has been determined that in this time, at this stage of the process of redemption, we are to be sacrifices of the agonies of the Messiah, that we are to go on the stake, happy are we that we have been given such meritorious opportunity. When our sages said: 'May he come, but let me not see!', this one may say only before the event — but we who have reached this stage must rejoice that our ashes will purify all Israel. I command you not to panic and not to weep as you go into the oven but rather to be joyous, with the song *Ani Ma'amin*, and like Rabbi Akiba to die with the word 'one' of the *Shema* on your lips". The people obeyed the words of the holy one, and singing *Ani Ma'amin* and reciting the *Shema Yisrael* they publicly sanctified God. May God keep them, and may their memory be blessed.
RELATED OF RABBI ISRAEL SHAPIRA OF GRADSIKS BY HIS SON

It was dark and frosty, pain congealed into ice
When the train took you away into the snowy distance,
Despair rapped at the walls, at the wind,
Hail like hardened tears beat on the lid of buried hope.

Again the mind poisoned self with bits of some reckoning,
With faded sympathies and unfinished rôles.
How bitter the draught of such memories.
Calm, my darling, I know how it hurts.

You were lonely, alone in the sombre throng
Though all there were tortured by the very same thoughts.
You are silent. No one understands you down at bottom.
Each is fenced off from the other by his own fate and pain.

MARTYROLOGY

So much suffering in each shadow here,
So much wrong hammered together here.
The blood flows, the hurt howls in impotent silence,
A poison-soaked ring throttles and eats at the vitals.

I know not where you are, or whether you still are —
You're still being carried by that same train
That carries us all — woefully tired and vanquished,
With battered heart and wounded spirit.

But calm, my darling, do not mar your blue eyes with tears,
Drive away the words of despair, accuse not even your fate.
It is all so very simple; we have all been thrown
To the crass and wicked epoch and doomed without mercy.

Soothe your aching heart. Others perish beside us,
Delivered to the same fate — in long unending queues ...
Morituri ... You know it. No need to deceive,
So I won't comfort you with words that are easy.

Be calm, my darling. What if over the cradle
A voice seemed to call to a different fate?
In our epoch the grave is life's closest neighbour.
Don't wrinkle, my darling, your saddened brow.

Into the pyramid of diabolical outrage
The future cuts strongly. Listen — but knowingly.
A tear will glisten in the eyes of those coming after us.
They will think of us quietly, profoundly.

The account is not closed yet. There is fire in the hand yet.
Despair is not for us, nor empty weakness.
Whether we die or live — no tear, no groan, my darling.
Clench your heart into your fists and your mouth — seal it firmly.

M. B. (AN UNIDENTIFIED POET WHO PERISHED IN THE NAZI
EXTERMINATION CAMPS)

I stand in awe before the memory of the *K'doshim* who walked into the gas chambers with the *Ani Ma'amin* — I believe! — on their lips. How dare I question, if they did not question. I believe because they believed. And I stand in awe before the *K'doshim*, before the memory of the untold suffering of innocent human beings who walked to the gas chambers without faith, because what was imposed upon them was more than man can endure. They could not believe any more — and now I do not know how to believe because I understand so well their disbelief. In fact, I find it easier to understand the loss of faith in the

MARTYROLOGY

"Kz" (concentration camps) than the faith preserved and affirmed. The faith affirmed was superhuman; the loss of faith — in the circumstances — human. Since I am only human, what is human is nearer to me than is the super-human. The faith is holy; but so are the disbelief and the religious rebellion of the concentration camps holy. The disbelief was not intellectual, but faith crushed, shattered, pulverized. And faith murdered a millionfold is holy disbelief. Those who were not there, and yet readily accept the Holocaust as the will of God that must not be questioned, desecrate the holy disbelief of those whose faith was murdered. And those who were not there and yet join with self-assurance the rank of the disbelievers, desecrate the holy faith of the believers.

One may, perhaps, go even further and say: The pious believer, who was not there, but who meekly submits, not to his own destruction, but to that of six million of his brethren, insults with his faith the faith of the concentration camps. The *K'doshim*, who affirmed their faith in the God of Israel in the light of the doom that surrounded them, may well say to such an eager believer: "What do you know about believing, about having faith? How dare you submit into suffering what is not yours? Calm down and be silent". But they, too, who were not there, and yet declare from the house-tops their disbelief in the God of Israel, insult the holy disbelief of the concentration camps. They who lost their faith there may well turn to our radical theologians: "How dare you speak about loss of faith, what do you know about losing faith, you who have never known what we have known, who never experienced what we have experienced!" In the presence of the holy faith of the crematoria, the ready faith of those who were not there is vulgarity. But the disbelief of the sophisticated intellectual in the midst of an affluent society — in the light of the holy disbelief of the crematoria — that is obscenity.

We are not Job and we dare not speak and respond as if we were. We are only Job's brother. We must believe, because our brother Job believed; and we must question, because our brother Job so often could not believe any more. This is not a comfortable situation; but is our condition in this era after the Holocaust. This must not be our last word. Rather, it is the very first one with which we stand at the threshold to an adequate response to the *Shoah* — if there be one. It is from this threshold alone that the break-in and the break-through must come. It must come without the desecration of the holy faith or of the holy loss of faith of the European hell of the Jewish people. And if there be no breakthrough, the honest thing is to remain living at the

MARTYROLOGY

threshold. If there is no answer, it is better to live without it than to find peace either in the sham of an insensitive faith or in the humbug of a disbelief that has eaten its fill.

ELIEZER BERKOVITS

There is a tradition about the old great Jewish community in Alexandria. It says that there was a Temple of such enormous size that on the High Holy Days there was no other possibility of conveying to the assembled faithful that the moment for pronouncing the "Amen" together had come than by waving a large flag which could be seen from all places. No flag would be large enough in order to create today such harmony of devoted communion in prayer, and even the flaming constellations of the stars would not be sufficient today, because our dispersion over the whole earth would demand too many differential hours during the day. But no distance is too large, no dispersion too great to stem the tide of the unity of will and hope which like a single large stream floods all Jewish hearts during these days. Festival time and world time give the great signals when and for what purpose "Amen" is to be said, this Amen which contains above all the promise of a Jewry united in hope and will, to help one another in the spirit of these days.

Perhaps the very differential of time which causes us to engage in the same thoughts around the whole earth may be encouraging in that for some Jewish communities the sun rises while for others it sinks. In one and the same hour some Jews have darkness, but others have light. Pure geographical happenstance, some will say. But who amongst us knows where geography ceases and history begins? Who amongst us doubts that our continued existence in this world has its origin in these necessary transitions which in retrospect one can draw in their clear outlines, but which cause the soul of the Jew to tremble if he has to experience it?

The power of a community to bear the burden of unfolding history depends on the depth of recognition of its own experienced destiny. History cannot be donned like a historic costume, not even in one's own community. But if we realize in how many costumes we have traversed the space of history we understand that we can cross the border-lines of epochs only as we cross them dressed clearly as Jews, — dressed not according to fashion but according to the experienced law of our existence.

CENTRALVEREIN ZEITSCHRIFT (ONE OF THE LAST ARTICLES PUBLISHED IN THIS JOURNAL OF THE MAJOR GERMAN JEWISH PROTECTIVE ORGANISATION BEFORE THE SECOND WORLD WAR.)

AVODAH – *The Ritual*

The *Avodah* (service, Temple worship) is the order of worship of the Israelites in the Temple. It is related during the Yom Kippur Musaph service in order to recall former glories and to re-enact symbolically the ancient rites ...

The High Priest made confession three times – once for himself, once for his household and the priests, and once for all the congregation of Israel. When making these confessions he would pronounce the "glorious and awful name", i.e. the ineffable name of God which could not be pronounced at any other time, and when the people and the priests heard it they fell upon their faces. When the Reader and congregation refer to the priests and the people prostrating themselves they, too, fall to the ground on their knees and touch the ground with their faces.

LOUIS JACOBS

The key verse in the Torah's enactment of the Yom Kippur rites is: "And he shall make atonement for the holy place, because of their transgressions, even all their sins; and so shall he do for the tent of meeting, that dwells with them in the midst of their uncleannesses", (*Lev 16:16*) ... The Sanctuary can be for us symbolic of the home, the synagogue, the school and other fundamental institutions of the community. These institutions, which should be the abode of God, are often contaminated by people's avarice and self-seeking. Even religious institutions need to be cleansed of corruption. Have not monumental cruelties been practised in the name of religion? Every one of us should therefore recognize his individual responsibility for the contamination of our social and religious institutions. Institutions are not buildings. They consist of people. Only a wholehearted recognition of our individual responsibility for the quality of our communal institutions will serve to restore the Divine Presence into our community life. Without such an atonement, our "sanctuaries" are in danger of becoming sacrilegious substitutes for authentic religion.

MAX ARZT

God's world is great and holy. The holiest land in the world is the Land of Israel. In the Land of Israel the holiest city is Jerusalem. In Jerusalem the holiest spot was the Holy of Holies.

There are seventy peoples in the world. The holiest among these is the People of Israel. The holiest of the People of Israel is the tribe of Levi. In the tribe of Levi the holiest are the priests. Among the priests the holiest was the High Priest.

AVODAH – *The Ritual*

There are 354 days in the year. Among these the holidays are holy. Higher than these is the holiness of the Sabbath. Among Sabbaths, the holiest is the Day of Atonement, the Sabbath of Sabbaths.

There are seventy languages in the world. The holiest is Hebrew. Holier than all else in this language is the holy Torah, and in the Torah the holiest part is the Ten Commandments. In the Ten Commandments the holiest of all words is the name of God.

And once during the year, at a certain hour, these four supreme sanctities of the world were joined with one another. That was on the Day of Atonement, when the High Priest would enter the Holy of Holies and there utter the name of God. And because this hour was beyond measure holy and awesome, it was the time of utmost peril not only for the High Priest but for the whole of Israel. For if in this hour there had, God forbid, entered the mind of the High Priest a false or sinful thought, the entire world would have been destroyed.

Every spot where a man raises his eyes to heaven, is a Holy of Holies. Every man, having been created by God in His own image and likeness, is a High Priest. Every day of a man's life is a Day of Atonement, and every word that a man speaks with sincerity is the name of the Lord. Therefore it is that every sin and every wrong that a man commits brings the destruction of the world ...

S. ANSKI

AVODAH – *Sacrifice*

So long as Judaism recognized the validity of the sacrificial service, the clear distinctiveness of the idea of atonement was subject to a certain limitation. As a visible act of penitence, the sin-offering plays the part of mediator between man and God. Though meant to serve as a bridge leading to the condoning God, in fact it came between man and his God. Rabbi Eleazar, living shortly after the destruction of the Temple, pronounced these bold words: "On the day when the Temple was destroyed there fell an iron wall, which had raised itself up between Israel and the Father in heaven". These were the words of a man who emphasized the fact that prayer was more than a sacrifice, that it was rather the inner emotion of devoutness which caused man to be united with God. From a somewhat later period comes a passage which can be matched by others: "The Torah says, Let the sinner bring a sin-offering, and he will obtain atonement; but God says, Let the sinner return, and he will obtain atonement" ... By the time of the destruction of the Temple, the best spirits of the community acknowledged that (animal) sacrifice was not essential for true atonement. The old

AVODAH – Sacrifice

prophetic idea that God "desired love and not sacrifice" (*Hosea 6:6*), that "the sacrifices of God are a contrite spirit" (*Psalms 51:14*), that God did not "command sacrifice" (*I Samuel 15:22*) but only "justice and righteousness" (*Jeremiah 7:21ff*) was reasserted with renewed strength. Once more it was seen that the atonement is the free ethical deed. "More than all sacrifices are beneficence, devotion, repentance, and the words of the Torah", "Return and good deeds", "return, doing good, and prayer" — these conceptions now formed a religious unity which became a permanent possession of the language of Judaism. By the substitution of the good deed which is the worship of God in actual life for an offering on the altar, the idea and ethical significance of the sacrificial service were retained intact. Sacrifice steps out of the Temple, the forecourt of life, into real life; atonement and repentance enter into their innermost sanctuary, the human heart.

LEO BAECK

To sacrifice is not to abandon what has been granted to us, to throw away the gifts of life. It is, on the contrary, giving back to God what we have received from Him by employing it in His service. Such giving is a form of thanksgiving ... The purpose of sacrifice does not lie in self-pauperization as such, but in the yielding of all aspirations to God, thus creating space for Him in the heart.

ABRAHAM JOSHUA HESCHEL

Whatever share, then, of the Divine favour we Jews enjoy we must win — win as all other men win it — by deserving it. But it is especially hard for us to win it. For a higher standard of obedience is exacted from us than is demanded from others, and by that does God judge us. A larger measure of self-renunciation, with all its attendant difficulty and pain — that is what our election means. Our consecration involves suffering, and is made effective only through suffering. For though we call ourselves God's people, we have to make good our right to the honoured title, and we cannot make it good save by victory over our lower selves. The Rabbis taught this truth. "God", they say, "gave three choice gifts to Israel — the Torah, the Land of Promise, and Eternal Life — and each was won by suffering". And the saying is always true. Whatever changes are in store for Israel, or for the external shape in which his religion expresses itself, the old ordinance which decrees self-sacrifice as the price of his election will abide. The Law will always be a yoke, though a glorious yoke; and the duty of bending beneath it in humble and glad self-surrender is the characteristic obligation of Israel through the ages.

MORRIS JOSEPH

AVODAH – *Sacrifice*

Shall I offer unto the Lord
That which has cost me nought,
That which I have not bought
For silver and gold at a price?
Shall I to God's altar bring
Thine oxen for offering?
Then Thine, not mine, were the sacrifice ...

Lord let me bring unto Thee
Prayers that true faith has wrought,
Self-sacrifice, dearly bought,
And patience, whose lamp never dies,
With penitence set apart;
For a broken and contrite heart
O Lord, Thou wilt not despise.

ALICE LUCAS

AVODAH – *Kneeling*

What distinguishes the Days of Awe from all other festivals is that here and only here does the Jew kneel. Here he does what he refused to do before the king of Persia, what no power on earth can compel him to do, and what he need not do before God on any other day of the year, or in any other situation he may face during his lifetime. And he does not kneel to confess a fault or to pray for forgiveness of sins, acts to which this festival is primarily dedicated. He kneels only in beholding the immediate nearness of God, hence on an occasion which transcends the earthly needs of today.

FRANZ ROSENZWEIG

MEMORIAL PRAYERS – *Meditations*

The son of a rabbi mourned the loss of his beloved father. Day after day he went to the cemetery and prostrated himself on the grave of his father. One day as the son gave way to paroxysms of sorrow, his father appeared to him in a vision and said: "My son, do you think that you honour my memory with your grief? Excessive grief is foolish. Do you think you truly express your love by your mourning? Offer me no tribute of tears. Build for me no monuments of sorrow. Do not weep for me. Live for me! Show your love by obedience to God's commandments, by devotion to your faith, and by service to your fellow man. This is the memorial that truly honours the departed".

MEMORIAL PRAYERS – *Meditations*

After hearing these words, the son lifted himself from his father's grave, and went forth to make of his father's memory a perpetual light to guide him on paths of righteousness and truth.

TALMUD

To My Mother

Other people say ordinary things
Like: "My mother used to spend hours
Unpicking string." Or:
"That trick of her old age
Nearly drove me to distraction."
I look at them
And try to comprehend
The simple action of remembering
Who have trained myself a childhood long
To forget so successfully.

What foibles were yours
That are now so forgotten,
My mother? Only I spend time in wondering
Who do not recall even the contours
Of a face I must have scanned
A thousand times in fear and hope,
A face that is now the skin of a lamp
Lit in the darkness of some insomniac's night;
Mine perhaps. You say all this is corny,
Or "prurient". No doubt it is fashionable.

Yet I cannot forget
What I do not remember
Now that no one thinks of you at all
But I who cannot think
Not remembering how once
You must have been young and cheerful,
Once even silly and giggly going to school,
Sick or delayed or in love and glad,
Who lie now with the sod, still and anonymous,
Burnt or gassed. Other methods often worked too.

I must surely understand that agony
Was not the totality of your life,
Nor evil the unambiguous sum
Of your appalling going.

MEMORIAL PRAYERS – *Meditations*
Then why should I who cannot remember
What you were nurse the residual wound
Of your mutilated absence
More than my neighbour who led you to die?
Must we all have atoned
For the crimes we are yet to commit?
HILDA SCHIFF

Strange now to think of you, gone without corsets and eyes, while
    I walk on the sunny pavement of Greenwich Village.
downtown Manhattan, clear winter noon, and I've been up
    all night, talking, talking, reading the Kaddish aloud,
    listening to Ray Charles blues shout blind on the
    phonograph the rhythm the rhythm — and your memory in my head
    three years after — And read Adonais' last triumphant stanzas
    aloud — wept, realising how we suffer —
And how Death is that remedy all singers dream of ...
... as I walk toward the
    Lower East Side — where you walked 50 years ago, little
    girl — from Russia, eating the first poisonous tomatoes
    of America — frightened on the dock —
then struggling in the crowds of Orchard Street toward what? —
    toward Newark —
toward candy store, first home-made sodas of the century, hand-
    churned ice cream in backroom on musty brownfloor
    boards —
Toward education marriage nervous breakdown, operation,
    teaching school, and learning to be mad, in a dream —
    what is this life?
ALLEN GINSBERG (FROM "KADDISH")

To you that build the new house.
    "There are stones like souls". Rabbi Nachman

When you come to put up your walls anew —
Your stove, your bedstead, table and chair —
Do not hang your tears for those who departed,
Who will not live with you then,
On to the stone.
Nor on the timber —
Else weeping will pierce the sleep,
The brief sleep you have yet to take.

MEMORIAL PRAYERS – *Meditations*

Do not sigh when you bed your sheets,
Else your dreams will mingle
With the sweat of the dead.

Oh, the walls and household utensils
Are responsive as Aeolian harps
Or like a field in which your sorrow grows,
And they sense your kinship with dust.

Build, when the hourglass trickles,
But do not weep away the minutes
Together with the dust
That obscures the light.

NELLY SACHS

Our Home with God

Our life is a narrow crumbling path
That we tread as we long have trod,
Ice and hail, valleys and precipice,
Till we come home at night to God.

We all of us carry heavy sacks,
Precious gems in some, in others a useless load.
But whatever we bear our backs are bent by the weight,
Till we come home at night to God.

Some hurry, some crawl, it makes no difference at all.
Your road is measured off, each yard, each rod,
Some go miles, some from the cradle but an inch or two,
Till the horizon ends and we are home with God.

My hours grow shorter, more brief my days.
I go about with other people's tread that I have borrowed.
Any moment the sky on my road may fall,
And I shall find myself at home with God.

JOSEPH ROLNIK

The road to the eternal is indicated to him; it never vanishes, not even in death, and never ceases to be his road. The direction of life and its depth stretch beyond the boundary of human existence. Over beginning and end remain abidingly the nearness of God, the eternal source and the eternal goal. The life of man means more than the narrowness of existence in this world. With all its deficiencies and limitations, its pain and suffering, it is, as the old Rabbinic metaphor says, but a place of "preparation", an "ante-chamber"; it is only the "life of the hour". The

MEMORIAL PRAYERS – *Meditations*

true life is the "eternal life". Man is created and destined to be different from the world, to be holy. As the image of God he belongs to that other, the higher life; he is a "child of the world to come". The spiritual, the good, is implanted in him as the strength, as the reality, of his existence, and this, the truly real of his life is exalted above death and destruction. His life remains life, even beyond death.
LEO BAECK

NEILAH

In Temple times deputations of laymen were delegated to be present each day when the priests offered up the sacrifices on behalf of Israel. Towards the end of the day when the Temple gates were about to be shut these men would recite the Prayer of the Closing of the Gates (*Neilath Shearim*) ... At a later period it was natural to associate the idea of the closing gates with the gates of Heaven open to prayer during the long day. The note sounded at *Neilah* is one of hope. The sun is about to set, the prayers have ascended on high, Israel has become reconciled to its God. The traditional melodies express the mood of longing, of yearning for a better life, of triumph over sin.
LOUIS JACOBS

For twenty-five hours the Jew has prayed out his heart and mind on the Day of Atonement. When evening comes and the long fast draws to a close, tens of thousands of words must have been spoken and sung. And yet somehow we still feel that we have not penetrated to the heart of the matter; there are further unspoken feelings buried in us and interior courts in God's palace which we have not yet entered. Therefore, we muster the remaining physical and spiritual forces left under our command and make one last desperate effort to descend into the human depths and to climb to the divine heights. But words have earlier proved futile. We cry out the *Shema* — we repeat "Praised is the Name of the glory of His Kingdom" three times — and we stammer, each time at a higher and, as it were, more urgent pitch seven times over the three Hebrew words: "The Lord, He is God". No longer is it the meaning of the words but rather their rhythm, the scream of the soul that squeezes through them, the hammering of their insistent repetition, in which we place our hope. And, as if even this last resort had failed, finally we abandon the human voice and verbal expression altogether. We reach for the *shofar* and blow one long, piercing shriek: *teki'ah gedolah* — "This, surely, must rend the heavens".
STEVEN S. SCHWARZSCHILD

NEILAH

The great Giver has ended His disposing;
the long day
is over and the gates are closing.
How badly all that has been read
was read by us,
how poorly all that should be said.

All wickedness shall go in smoke.
It must, it must!
The just shall see and be glad.
The sentence is sweet and sustaining;
for we, I suppose, are the just;
and we, the remaining.

If only I could write with four pens between five fingers
and with each pen a different sentence at the same time —
but the rabbis say it is a lost art, a lost art.
I well believe it. And at that of the first twenty sins that
 we confess,
five are by speech alone;
little wonder that I must ask the Lord to bless
the words of my mouth and the meditations of my heart.

Now, as from the dead, I revisit the earth and delight
in the sky, and hear again
the noise of the city and see
earth's marvelous creatures — men.
Out of nothing I became a being,
and from a being I shall be
nothing — but until then
I rejoice, a mote in Your world,
a spark in Your seeing.
CHARLES REZNIKOFF

I find the meaning of *halachah* (Law, "walking") expressed with particular poignancy in the order of worship which requires that the daily evening prayer is to be said immediately upon the conclusion of the Neilah service on Yom Kippur. The Jew has prayed and fasted throughout the entire day. Now the day is ended. Everyone is eager to go home and break the fast. People are rushing out. Yet there is always at least a small group of persons who remain behind to recite the regular daily evening prayer. Having just cleansed and purified themselves, they again pronounce the daily bid for forgiveness. The Jewish year — time — has no pauses. *Halachah* governs the totality of man's life and time.
ERNST SIMON

BEFORE THE LAW

"Before the Law stands a doorkeeper on guard. To this doorkeeper there comes a man from the country who begs for admittance to the Law. But the doorkeeper says that he cannot admit the man at the moment. The man, on reflection, asks if he will be allowed, then, to enter later. 'It is possible', answers the doorkeeper, 'but not at this moment'. Since the door leading into the Law stands open as usual and the doorkeeper steps to one side, the man bends down to peer through the entrance. When the doorkeeper sees that, he laughs and says: 'If you are so strongly tempted, try to get in without my permission. But note that I am powerful. And I am only the lowest doorkeeper. From hall to hall keepers stand at every door, one more powerful than the other. Even the third of these has an aspect that even I cannot bear to look at'. These are difficulties which the man from the country has not expected to meet, the Law, he thinks, should be accessible to every man and at all times, but when he looks more closely at the doorkeeper in his furred robe, with his huge pointed nose and long, thin, Tartar beard, he decides that he had better wait until he gets permission to enter. The doorkeeper gives him a stool and lets him sit down at the side of the door. There he sits waiting for days and years. He makes many attempts to be allowed in and wearies the doorkeeper with his importunity. The doorkeeper often engages him in brief conversation, asking him about his home and about other matters, but the questions are put quite impersonally, as great men put questions, and always conclude with the statement that the man cannot be allowed to enter yet. The man, who has equipped himself with many things for his journey, parts with all he has, however valuable, in the hope of bribing the doorkeeper. The doorkeeper accepts it all, saying, however, as he takes each gift: 'I take this only to keep you from feeling that you have left something undone'. During all these long years the man watches the doorkeeper almost incessantly. He forgets about the other doorkeepers, and this one seems to him the only barrier between himself and the Law. In the first years he curses his evil fate aloud; later, as he grows old, he only mutters to himself. He grows childish, and since in his prolonged watch he has learned to know even the fleas in the doorkeeper's fur collar, he begs the very fleas to help him and to persuade the doorkeeper to change his mind. Finally his eyes grow dim and he does not know whether the world is really darkening around him or whether his eyes are only deceiving him. But in the darkness he can now perceive the radiance that streams immortally from the door of

BEFORE THE LAW

the Law. Now his life is drawing to a close. Before he dies, all that he has experienced during the whole time of his sojourn condenses in his mind into one question, which he has never put to the doorkeeper. He beckons the doorkeeper, since he can no longer raise his stiffening body. The doorkeeper has to bend far down to hear him, for the difference in size between them has increased very much to the man's disadvantage. 'What do you want to know now?' asks the doorkeeper, 'you are insatiable'. 'Everyone strives to attain the Law', answers the man, 'how does it come about, then, that in all these years no one has come seeking admittance but me?' The doorkeeper perceives that the man is at the end of his strength and that his hearing is failing, so be bellows in his ear: 'No one but you could gain admittance through this door, since this door was intended only for you. I am now going to shut it'".

FRANZ KAFKA

GLOSSARY

ABRAHAMS, ISRAEL. (1858-1925) Reader in Talmudics at Cambridge, early leader of the Liberal Jewish movement. Author of *"Jewish Life in the Middle Ages"* and an explanatory companion to Singer's Prayer Book.

AGNON, SHMUEL YOSEPH. (1888-1970) Born in Poland, migrated to Palestine in 1907. Considered the greatest contemporary Hebrew writer of fiction. Shared Nobel Prize for literature in 1966 with *Nelly Sachs.

AHAI GAON. (died c. 762) First rabbinical author after the close of the Talmud. Wrote *Sheeltot* ("questions"), legal material arranged according to the Pentateuch.

AKIBA BEN JOSEPH. (c. 50-c. 135 CE) Most prominent among *Tannaim. Began to study late in life, introduced systematisation of law and developed new methods for interpreting Bible. Supported Bar Kochba's rebellion and died as a martyr.

ALBO, JOSEPH. (c. 1380-c. 1435) Spanish preacher, philosopher and apologist. Author of *Sefer Halkkarim* (*"Book of Dogmas"*).

ALMEMOR. Elevated platform in Synagogue on which the desk stands for reading from the Scroll.

AMORA, pl. AMORAIM. "Speaker" "interpreter", masters of the second talmudic epoch (about 200-500 CE) in which the *Gemara originates.

ANI MA'AMIN. "I believe" – the opening words of a song of faith in the coming of the Messiah.

ANSKI, S. (SOLOMON SAMUEL RAPPAPORT). (1863-1920) Russian-Yiddish author and dramatist. Socialist revolutionary, author of the Bundist hymn *"The Oath"*. Wrote *"The Dybbuk"*.

ARZT, MAX. (1897-) American Conservative Rabbi. Born in Poland. Professor of practical theology at the Jewish Theological Seminary, New York. Author of *"Justice and Mercy, a Commentary on the New Year and the Day of Atonement"*.

AVODAH ZARAH. (Idolatry). Eighth tractate of the *Mishnah, order *Nezikin* (damages). Deals with idols and relations with idol-worshippers.

AVOT D'RABBI NATHAN. A small tractate, usually printed with the Babylonian *Talmud. Midrashic commentaries to the *Sayings of the Fathers.

BAAL SHEM TOV. "Master of the Good Name". (ISRAEL BEN ELIEZER, BESHT). (c. 1700-1760) Founder of *Chasidism. Stressed the joyful observance of commandments and popularised Kabbalistic teachings.

BABA BATHRA. (Last Part) Third part of the first tractate of the *Mishnah, order *Nezikin* (damages). Deals mainly with real estate, inheritance and legal documents.

BACHYA IBN PAKUDA. (c. 1050-1120) Spanish, religious philosopher. His *"Duties of the Heart"* speaks of trust in God, humility and asceticism. Strong affinity with Arab mystics.

BAECK, LEO. (1873-1956) Rabbi, teacher of *Midrash and Homiletics in Berlin (Hochschule für die Wissenschaft des Judentums). Elected head of the representative council of the Jews in Germany in 1933, and stayed with his congregation until sent to Theresienstadt in 1943. Survived the war and settled in London. Books include *"The Essence of Judaism"* and *"This People Israel"*.

BARAITHA. Term for teachings of the *Tannaim not included in the *Mishnah.

BELKIN, SAMUEL. (1911-) Born Poland, settled in America 1929. Orthodox Rabbi, scholar in field of Jewish Hellenism. In 1947 became president of Yeshiva University.

GLOSSARY

BELLOW, SAUL. (1915-) American novelist whose Jewish characters search for ultimate reality in the modern world.

BEN SIRA, JESHUA. (JESUS BEN SIRACH). Author of a collection of wisdom materials for the religious and moral instruction of the young, preserved in the Apocrypha and known by its latin title Ecclesiasticus. Written in hebrew in Jerusalem about 190-170 BCE.

BERACHOT. (Blessings) First tractate of the *Mishnah, order *Zeraim* (seeds). Deals with the recitation of the Shema, and blessings and prayers in general.

BERDITZCHEVER. (See Levi Yitzhak of Berditzchev).

BERGMAN, SAMUEL HUGO. (1883-) Czech Zionist and philosopher (Hebrew University). Influenced by Ahad Ha-Am and *Buber.

BERKOWITZ, ELIEZER. (1900-) Born in Transylvania, ordained at the Hildesheimer Rabbinical Seminary. Left Germany 1939, reached America 1958 after serving in England (Leeds) and Australia. Modern Orthodox theologian and zionist.

BESHT. (See Baal Shem Tov).

BETTELHEIM, BRUNO. (1903-) Born in Vienna. Psychoanalyst. Imprisoned in Dachau and Buchenwald, now lives in America. Author of *"The Informed Heart"*.

BLUE, LIONEL. (1930-) British Rabbi. Educated Oxford, Leo Baeck College. Co-editor of the revision of the prayer books of the Reform Synagogues of Great Britain. Author of *"To Heaven with Scribes and Pharisees"*.

BOOK OF MORALS. 15th Century ethical work.

BRAUDE, WILLIAM GORDON. (1907-) American Rabbi and scholar. Born Telz, Lithuania, taken to U.S.A. in 1920. Author of translation of, and critical notes on, *Pesikta Rabbati* and the *Midrash on Psalms*.

BUBER, MARTIN. (1878-1965) Writer and philosopher from Vienna. In *"I and Thou"* saw faith as dialogue between man and God. Explored and popularised *Chasidism. Zionist and passionate advocate of Jewish-Arab understanding.

CHAGIGA. (Feast offering) Twelfth tractate of *Mishnah, order *Moed* (seasons). Deals with private offerings on the three pilgrim feasts.

CHASIDIC, CHASIDISM. A religious and social movement which developed quickly in depressed E. Europe following the Chmielnicki massacre and church persecution. It has parallels with other popular religious movements of the same period.

DANIEL, YULI. (1925-) Son of Russian-Jewish revolutionary writer Mordechai Meyerovich (Mark Daniel). Poet, translator and satirist. Imprisoned 1966 following notorious trial with fellow writer Andrey Sinyavsky. Released 1970, exiled from Moscow.

DE HAAN, JACOB ISRAEL. (1881-1924) Born Holland. Poet. Returned via Zionism to ultra-orthodoxy. 1919 emigrated to Palestine – but disliked by Jews and Arabs alike for his political and ideological affiliations. Murdered in Jerusalem.

DEUTERONOMY RABBAH. (See *Midrash Rabbah).

DOBRUSHIN, YECHEZKEL. (1883-1953) Born in Ukraine. Yiddish poet, literary critic and playwright. Held chair in Yiddish literature at the Yiddish State University, Kiev. Arrested when Jewish Anti-Fascist committee liquidated in 1948. Died in Siberian prison camp.

ECCLESIASTES RABBAH. (See *Midrash Rabbah).

EDUYOT. (Testimonies) Seventh tractate of *Mishnah, order *Nezikin* (damages). A collection of traditional laws and decisions given by earlier teachers.

ELEAZAR BEN PEDAT. (Third Century CE) *Amora. Born in Babylon, became acting Principal of the talmudical school at Tiberias.

GLOSSARY

ELEAZAR BEN SIMEON. (Second Century CE) *Tanna. Authority on rabbinical law, but censured for collaborating with the Romans, which he later regretted.

ELEAZAR ROKEACH (BEN JUDAH BEN KALONYMOS OF WORMS). (c. 1170-1238) Born in Mayence. Talmudist, mystic and hymn-writer. Best known work is *Sefer HaRokeach ("Book of the Perfumer")* on law and ethics. (The letters of the word "Rokeach" have the same numerical value as "Eleazar").

ELIJAH BEN RAPHAEL OF VEALI SABA. (1738-1792) Italian Kabbalist and poet. Rabbi of Alessandria.

ELIMELECH OF LIZENSK. (1717-1787) Popular leader of the third generation of *Chasidim, one of the founders of Chasidism in Galicia. Brother of *Zusya of Hanipol.

EXODUS RABBAH. (See *Midrash Rabbah).

FLEG, EDMOND. (1874-1963) French poet, playwright and essayist who returned to Judaism after the Dreyfus affair. Author of *"Why I am a Jew"* and *"Moses"*

FRANK, ANNE. (1929-1945) Born in Germany, grew up in Holland, and died in Belsen. Her diaries record the German occupation of Amsterdam.

FRANKL, VIKTOR E. (1905-) Psychiatrist, born in Austria. His ideas concerning purpose and meaning in life developed out of his experience in Auschwitz and other concentration camps.

FREUD, SIGMUND. (1856-1939) Founder of psychoanalysis, born in Vienna. Refugee in London in 1938.

GAON "eminence". Title of the heads of the Babylonian academies from the 6th to 11th Centuries.

GEMARA. (See *Mishnah).

GENESIS RABBAH. (See *Midrash Rabbah).

GERONDI, JONAH BEN ABRAHAM. (d. 1263) Spanish rabbi and moralist. Came from Gerona in Catalonia, died in Toledo. His *Shaarei Teshuvah ("Gates of Repentance")* is one of the standard Jewish ethical works of the middle ages.

GINSBERG, ALLEN. (1926-) American poet, leader of the "Beat generation". Draws hallucinatory pictures of alienation in contemporary America. Wrote the long poem *"Kaddish"* after the death of his mother.

GINZBURG, NATALIA. (1917-) Italian novelist and playwright. Her first husband, a victim of the Nazis, died in a Roman prison in 1944.

GOLDIN, JUDAH. (1914-) American scholar and teacher. Particularly concerned with rabbinic Judaism. Author of *"The Living Talmud"* a collection of commentaries on the *Sayings of the Fathers.

GOLLANCZ, VICTOR. (1893-1967) British Publisher, writer, socialist and humanitarian. Early fighter of Nazism. Organised relief from starvation in Germany in 1945 and relief work for Arabs during the Arab-Israel war. Governor of the Hebrew University.

GOULSTON, MICHAEL. (1932-1972) British Rabbi and educator. Minister at West London Synagogue, founder editor of European Judaism. The Michael Goulston Educational Foundation continues his pioneer work in new methods for Jewish education.

GREENBERG, CHAIM. (1889-1953) Labour Zionist theoretician. Born in Russia, worked in America.

HALACHAH. Literally "walking", term for Jewish law.

HALEVI, JUDAH. (c. 1075-1141) Spanish hebrew poet and philosopher. A physician who in old age left Spain to settle in Palestine during the period of the second crusade. Author of *"The Kuzari"*.

GLOSSARY

HARRISON, HOWARD. Contemporary American poet.

HECHASID, JUDAH. (1150-1217) Of Regensberg. Reputed to be a mystic. Little is known of him. Associated with * *Sefer Chasidim*.

HEIMLER, EUGENE. (1922-) Poet, psychiatric social worker. Born in Hungary, was in Auschwitz and other concentration camps. Came to England in 1947. The camp experiences are recalled in *"Night of the Mist"*, his subsequent recovery in *"A Link in the Chain"*.

HEINE, HEINRICH. (1797-1856) German poet and writer, born Jewish but baptised in 1825. After a serious illness in 1847 he increasingly returned to Jewish themes, particuiarly the Bible.

HERTZ, JOSEPH H. (1872-1946) Chief Rabbi of Great Britain for over thirty years. Editor of standard commentary on Pentateuch and the Prayer Book.

HESCHEL, ABRAHAM JOSHUA. (1902-1972) American Conservative Rabbi, philosopher and theologian. His works include *"God in Search of Man"*, *"The Sabbath"* and *"The Prophets"*.

HILLEL. (First Century BCE) Born in Babylonia, studied in Jerusalem. Became leading authority in Oral Law. Developed principles of Biblical interpretation, renowned for his humanity and ethical teachings.

HIMMELFARB, MILTON. Contemporary American writer. Editor of *American Jewish Year Book*, and contributing editor to *Commentary*.

HIRSCH, SAMSON RAPHAEL. (1808-1888) Leader of "orthodoxy" in Frankfurt. Tried to fuse western culture with orthodox Judaism. Author of commentaries on Pentateuch and Psalms, and *"Nineteen Letters"*.

IBN EZRA, MOSES. (c. 1060-c. 1139) Born in Granada. Poet, philosopher and philologist. Wrote in Hebrew and Arabic.

IBN GABIROL, SOLOMON. (c. 1021-1056) Spanish poet and philosopher. His *Keter Malchut ("Crown of Kingship")* is read during the Ten Days of Penitence.

JACOB BEN ASHER. (d. 1340) Spanish talmudist, codifier and Bible commentator. Author of code *Arbah Turim ("Four Columns")* aimed at bridging gap between Franco-German and Spanish rabbinical schools of Jewish law.

JACOBS, ARTHUR. (1937-) British poet and translator.

JACOBS, LOUIS. (1920-) English Rabbi and theologian. Lecturer in Talmud at Leo Baeck College. Works include *"We Have Reason To Believe"*, *"Chasidic Prayer"*, *"Principles of the Jewish Faith"*, etc.

JOSEPH, MORRIS. (1848-1934) English theologian and Rabbi of the West London Synagogue from 1893. His *"Judaism as Creed and Life"*, emphasising the ethical basis of Jewish observance, remains a standard work.

JUDAH BEN ASHER. (1270-1349) Born Germany, died Toledo where he was Rabbi. Talmudist, son of famous Talmudic authority Asher ben Yechiel (the *Rosh*) and brother of *Jacob ben Asher.

KAFKA, FRANZ. (1883-1924) Czech author whose works depict the fear and despair of western man. Works include *"The Trial"*, *"The Castle"* and many aphorisms.

K'DOSHIM. "The holy ones" — term used for all who died as martyrs for "Kiddush HaShem", the sanctification of the name of God.

KIDDUSHIN. Seventh tractate of the *Mishnah, order *Nashim* (women), dealing with betrothal and prohibited marriages.

KITZUR SHULCHAN ARUCH, SHULCHAN ARUCH. (*The Prepared Table*) By Joseph Caro (1488-1575). An authoritative code of Jewish law and practice. The Kitzur Shulchan Aruch is a simplified edition by Solomon Ganzfried (1804-1886).

KOOK, ABRAHAM ISAAC. (RAV KOOK). (1865-1935) Chief Rabbi of Palestine, concerned with the religious problems of the new settlement. Legal authority, poet and mystic.

GLOSSARY

KRAUS, KARL. (1874-1936) Austrian satirist and poet.

LAMENTATIONS RABBAH. (See *Midrash Rabbah).

LANDAU, ZISHA. (1889-1937) Yiddish poet. Born Poland, settled in America 1906. One of the leaders of the "Younger" group in Yiddish poetry in America.

LEOVER, DOV (OF LEOVO). (1827-1876) Son of Israel of Rushin of the Rushin Chasidic dynasty..Published an attack on chasidism which caused fierce controversy between the dynasties of Zandz and Sadgora, unresolved by his own later repentance.

LEVITICUS RABBAH. (See *Midrash Rabbah).

LEVI YITZHAK OF BERDITZCHEV. (THE BERDITZCHEVER). (1740-1809) Chasidic leader, pupil of Dov Baer of Mezritch. Central doctrine was "love for Israel".

LIEBERMAN, CHAIM. (1890-1963) Born Volhynia, lived in New York from 1908. Yiddish literary critic and essayist.

LUCAS, ALICE. (1852-1935) English poetess. Translator of mediaeval liturgical poetry.

LURIA, ISAAC. (1534-1572) Kabbalist and mystic who settled in Safed. His great contribution to Jewish though is his amplification of the idea of *kavanah* (intention).

LUZZATTO, MOSES CHAIM. (1707-1747) Born Padua. Mystic, poet, scholar. Forerunner of the modern Hebrew revival. Author of the ethical work *Mesilat Yesharim* ("Path of the Upright"). His mystical works led to persecution and excommunication. Found refuge in Amsterdam, died in Acre.

MAASEY BOOK. Popular mediaeval collection of legends and stories in Yiddish.

MAHARAL OF PRAGUE (THE GREAT RABBI JUDAH LOEW BEN BEZALEL). (c. 1512-1609) Talmudist, Mathematician. Legendary creator of the Golem.

MAIMONIDES, MOSES. (MOSES BEN MAIMON, RaMBaM). (1135-1204) Philosopher, halachist, physician. Born Cordova, finally settled in Cairo where he became spiritual head of the community. Wrote the *Mishnah Torah* – a code covering all halachic subjects discussed in the Talmud, and *"Guide for the Perplexed"*, an exposition of Judaism's basic teachings, influenced by Aristotelian thought.

MARMORSTEIN, ARTHUR. (1882-1946) Born in Hungary. Studied at Rabbinic seminaries of Budapest and Berlin. From 1912 taught at Jew's College. Important studies in rabbinic theology include *"The Old Rabbinic Doctrine of God"*.

MASHGIACH. Overseer, supervisor.

MAYBAUM, IGNAZ. (1897-) Rabbi. Refugee from Nazis. First lecturer in Theology and Comparative Religion at the Leo Baeck College. Author of several books, including: *"The Synagogue and Society", "Trialogue between Jew, Christian and Muslim", "The Face of God After Auschwitz".*

MENES, A. (1888-) Born in Lithuania, prominent in Bundist movement. Since 1946 in New York. Editorial contributor to Yiddish daily paper.

MEZUZAH. Symbol on the doorpost of a Jewish house containing the first two paragraphs of the *Shema.

MIDRASH. The finding of new meaning, in addition to the literal one, of Biblical texts. Sometimes midrash teaches law (*halachah*) at other times myths, legends, ethics, parables, etc. (*aggadah*).

MIDRASH PROVERBS. (See *Midrash Rabbah).

MIDRASH PSALMS. (See *Midrash Rabbah).

MIDRASH RABBAH. A collection of midrashim on the Pentateuch and the five *Megillot* (scrolls) – Song of Songs, Ruth, Lamentations, Ecclesiastes, Esther. The books stem from different periods and differ among themselves in their general character.

GLOSSARY

MINYAN. "Quorum", the minimum number, ten males over the age of thirteen, traditionally required for public worship.

MISHNAH. Legal codification of the Oral Law, compiled by Rabbi Judah HaNasi, 2nd Century CE. It is divided into six orders — a) *Zeraim* (seeds) dealing primarily with agricultural laws, but also containing the rules of prayer; b) *Moed* (seasons) dealing with the Sabbath, Festivals, etc.; c) *Nashim* (women) dealing with marriage, divorce and vows; d) *Nezikin* (damages) dealing with civil and criminal legislation; e) *Kedoshim* (holy things) dealing with the laws of slaughter, sacrifice and consecrated objects; f) *Taharot* (purities) dealing with laws of ritual purity. Each order is then subdivided, forming a total of 66 tractates, which are then further treated in the *Gemara*. Mishnah and Gemara together make up the *Talmud.

MONTEFIORE, CLAUDE GOLDSMID. (1859-1939) English scholar, concerned with the New Testament period, and a founder of the Liberal Jewish movement in England.

MORDECHAI OF NADVORNA. (d. 1896) Chasidic leader.

MOSES BEN JACOB OF COUCY. (SeMaG). (13th Century) French talmudist and codifier of the 613 mitzvot in his work *Sefer Mitzvot HaGadol*. Took part in a disputation in Paris in 1240 in defence of the Talmud.

NACHMANIDES. (MOSES BEN NACHMAN, RaMBaN). (c. 1195-c. 1270) Born in Gerona. Physician, talmudist, mystic and Bible interpreter. Compelled to have a public disputation with Pablo Christiani, a convert to Christianity, in 1267, at the court of Barcelona. Died in Acre.

NACHMAN OF BRATZLAV. (1772-1811) Chasidic rabbi and ascetic — great-grandson of the *Besht. His stories and parables exalt the importance of the *tzaddik* (righteous man).

NEWMAN, JEFFREY. (1941-) British Rabbi. Educated Oxford and Leo Baeck College.

NUMBERS RABBAH. (See *Midrash Rabbah).

PELZ, WERNER AND LOTTE. (Born c. 1920) As Jewish refugee children settled in England. Concerned with Judaism, Bible and modern thought. Co-authors of *"God is no More", "True Deceivers"*.

PERETZ, ISAAC LEIBUSH. (1852-1915) Polish short-story writer and essayist. Considered "the father" of modern Yiddish literature.

PESACHIM. (Paschal lambs, Passover-offerings). Third tractate of *Mishnah, order *Moed* (seasons). Deals with laws relating to the feast of Passover and the paschal lamb.

PESIKTA D'RAV KAHANA. Collection of midrashic sermons for the holidays and special Sabbaths of the year. Probably 7th Century.

PESIKTA RABBATI. Collection of midrashic sermons for the holidays and special Sabbaths. Contains different material to *Pesikta d'rav Kahana. Probably 7th Century.

PETUCHOWSKI, JAKOB JOSEF. (1925-) Born in Berlin, emigrated to England before 1939. Ordained from Hebrew Union College, where he is now professor of rabbinics. Author of *"Understanding Jewish Prayer"*.

PREMSLA, MOSES BEN ABRAHAM. (16 Century) Author of *Matteh Moshe ("The Staff of Moses")*, a liturgical compendium printed in Cracow 1571.

RATHENAU, MATHILDE NACHMAN. Mother of Walter Rathenau. When the mother of her son's murderer was subjected to public insults, she wrote her a letter of consolation.

REISEN, ABRAHAM. (1876-1953) Russian. One of most popular Yiddish writers and poets. Settled in America 1908.

GLOSSARY

REZNIKOFF, CHARLES. (1894-) American poet and lawyer. Selected edition of his poems published as *"By the Waters of Manhattan"*.

RODIN, ELISHA. (1885-1946) Born in Moscow, published poetry in Yiddish from 1913. Began writing in Hebrew when that language was proscribed. A collection of lyrical eulogies on the death of his son was published in Palestine in 1943 while he was imprisoned in a Siberian labour camp where he died.

ROLNIK, JOSEPH. (1879-1955) Russia. Yiddish poet, emigrated to America in 1899.

ROSENZWEIG, FRANZ. (1886-1929) German philosopher, born of an assimilated family, who came close to converting to Christianity, but then rediscovered Judaism and spent the rest of his life in Jewish education. Translated large part of the Bible into German together with *Martin Buber. Author of *"The Star of Redemption"*.

ROSH HASHANAH. (New Year). Eighth tractate of *Mishnah, order *Moed* (seasons). Deals with New Year.

ROTH, LEON. (1894-1963) Philosopher. Professor at the Hebrew University, 1928-1953. Influential in starting and endowing Leo Baeck College.

RUTH RABBAH. (See *Midrash Rabbah).

SAADIAH GAON. (892-942) Born Fayyum, Egypt, settled in Babylon and appointed *Gaon of Sura. Wrote books on grammar, exegesis, philosophy, halachah and liturgy. Leader in struggle against Karaism.

SACHS, NELLY. (1891-1970) German poet and playwright. Assimilated background, she rediscovered her Jewish heritage after 1933. Her reputation based on her post-war works depicting the holocaust. Shared Nobel Prize for Literature in 1966 with *S. Y. Agnon.

SANHEDRIN. (Court of Justice). Fourth tractate of the *Mishnah, order *Nezikin* (damages), dealing with courts of justice and judicial procedures, particularly criminal law and punishments.

SAYINGS OF THE FATHERS. (PIRKE AVOT). Tractate of the *Mishnah with no talmudic commentary. Contains sayings of Rabbis and teachers from the 3rd Century BCE to the 3rd Century CE.

SCHECHTER, SOLOMON. (1850-1915) Founder of Conservative Judaism. Lecturer in *Talmud at Cambridge, discoverer of a *Genizah* (store) of ancient Hebrew literature in Egypt. President of the Jewish Theological Seminary in New York.

SCHIFF, HILDA. Contemporary writer and poetess.

SCHMELKE OF NIKOLSBURG. (d. 1778) Chasidic leader, disciple of Dov Baer of Mezritch.

SCHNITZLER, ARTHUR. (1862-1931) Austrian dramatist and novelist. Interested in psychology and antisemitism.

SCHOENBERG, ARNOLD. (1874-1951) Austrian composer, protégé of Mahler. Returned to Judaism and wrote the opera *"Moses and Aaron"*, music to the psalms and a setting of Kol Nidre.

SCHWARTZ, ISRAEL JACOB. (1885-) Lithuania. Emigrated to America 1906. Yiddish poet, translated *"Paradise Lost"* into Yiddish.

SCHWARZSCHILD, STEVEN S. Contemporary American philosopher. Former editor of *"Judaism"*, Professor of Philosophy and Judaic Studies at Washington University, St. Louis.

SCHWEID, MARK. (1891-) Polish-born Yiddish poet. Emigrated to America in 1911. Actor, playwright, novelist and translator.

SEDER ELIAHU RABBAH. (TANNA DEVE ELIYAHU). *Midrash in two parts, probably 9th Century, Italy, but perhaps earlier.

GLOSSARY

SEFER CHASIDIM (See Judah Hechasid). (*"Book of the Pious"*). Ethical teachings of the *Chasidei Ashkenaz*, a German pietistic movement of the 12th and early 13th Centuries.

SEFER HACHINUCH. (*"Book of Education"*) Earliest book of religious instruction among the Jews of the middle ages. By Aaron HaLevi, a Spanish talmudist, end of 13th Century.

SEGAL, I. I. (1896-1954) Born in Ukraine. Lived in New York from 1923. Wrote poetry in Yiddish, Russian and Hebrew.

SELICHOT. (From a root meaning "to pardon"). Penitential prayers recited before the morning service in the days before Rosh Hashanah and during the Ten Days of Penitence.

SHABBAT. (Sabbath) First tractate of the *Mishnah, order *Moed* (seasons), dealing with the rules of the Sabbath and its observance, including the 39 categories of prohibited work.

SHECHINAH. The presence of God.

SHEKALIM. (Shekels). Fourth tractate of *Mishnah, order *Moed* (seasons), dealing with the half Shekel which every Israelite had to pay as temple tax.

SHELOMO OF KARLIN. (d. 1792) Chasidic leader, disciple of Dov Baer of Mezritch.

SHEMA. One of central parts of Jewish prayer affirming the Oneness of God. It comprises three paragraphs: *Deut 6:4-9; 11:13-21; Numbers 15:37-41*. Reciting the first paragraph, the speaker accepts upon himself "the yoke of the kingdom of heaven".

SHIMMEL, MOSHE. (1904-) Lemberg. Polish Poet, turned to writing in Yiddish.

SHOAH. "Destruction". Hebrew term for the Holocaust.

SHUL. Yiddish for "School". Popular term for Synagogue.

SHULCHAN ARUCH. (See Kitzur Shulchan Aruch)

SIDLOVTZER, NATHAN DAVID. (d. 1865) Chasidic leader, son of Yerachmiel of Pzhysha (Parsischa).

SIFRA. (The Book). Halachic *Midrash on Leviticus.

SIFRE. (The Books). *Midrash on Numbers and Deuteronomy.

SIMEON BEN LAKISH (RESH LAKISH). (c. 200-c. 275) Palestinian *Amora. Renowned for his great strength (as a young man he was a gladiator or soldier). Independent line in legal matters and bible interpretation.

SIMMONS, VIVIAN GEORGE. (1885-1970) British. Studied at the Hochschule für die Wissenschaft des Judentums in Berlin and at Heidelberg. Minister of West London Synagogue, 1914-1940, and other Reform and Liberal congregations.

SIMON, ERNST. (1899-) Educator, religious thinker, writer. Born in Berlin, became active Zionist in 1918. Joined *Buber in struggle for Arab-Jewish understanding. Settled in Palestine 1928. Professor Emeritus of Education at Hebrew University.

SOLOVEICHIK, JOSEPH DOV BER OF BRISK. (1820-1892) Of the famous Lithuanian rabbinical family. Talmudist and head of the Yeshivah in Volozhin. Later settled in Brisk (Brest-Livosk) as communal leader. Much concerned with welfare work and charity.

SONG OF SONGS RABBAH. (See *Midrash Rabbah).

SPERBER, SHMUEL. Contemporary Czech. Rabbi, refugee in England. Jewish educationalist. Lives in Jerusalem.

STEINBERG, MILTON. (1903-1950) American conservative Rabbi. Books include *"The Making of the Modern Jew", "Basic Judaism"*.

GLOSSARY

STEINSALZ, ADIN. Contemporary Israeli Rabbi, scholar and mystic. Editor of new hebrew commentary on the *Talmud.

SUCCAH (Booth). Sixth tractate of *Mishnah, order *Moed* (seasons), dealing with laws concerning the feast of Tabernacles.

TA'ANIT (Fast). Ninth tractate of the *Mishnah, order *Moed* (seasons), dealing with special fasts, for example at a time of drought.

TALMON, JACOB LEIB. (1916-) Born in Poland, went to Palestine in 1934. Since 1960 Professor of History at the Hebrew University. Advocate of Jewish and Palestinian-Arab right of self-determination.

TALMUD (Teaching). Name applied to the *Mishnah with its *Gemara* (later commentary and supplement). Most of the tractates of the Mishnah have this commentary. Two versions of Talmud; one compiled in Palestine (the *Yerushalmi*), completed about 400 CE; the other in Babylon (the *Bavli*) completed about 100-300 years later.

TANCHUMA. Homiletic *Midrash on the Pentateach.

TANNA, TANNAIM. Rabbis, teachers of the oral law, who lived before the completion of the *Mishnah.

TOSEFTA. (Addition, Supplement). Mainly collections of laws not included in the *Mishnah, to which it forms a complement. It is similarly divided into 60 divisions. Contains also decisions and saying of later teachers of Babylonian and Palestinian schools. 5-6th Century CE.

VAN DER ZYL, WERNER. (1902-) Born in Schwerte, Westphalia. Graduated from the Hochschule für die Wissenschaft des Judentums in 1933. Served in Berlin until 1939, then moved to England at the urging of *Leo Baeck. Worked with refugee children before accepting the pulpit at the North Western Reform Synagogue (1943-1958) and West London Synagogue till his retirement in 1968. One of the initiators, and first Director of Studies, of the Leo Baeck College.

VIDUI. Confession of sins.

VIEVIORKA, ABRAHAM. (1887-1935) Born Poland, lived in London writing for and editing Yiddish periodicals. Went to Russia 1919, died in Kiev. Poet and dramatist.

VORKER, MENDEL. (MENACHEM MENDEL OF VORKI). (d. 1868) Chasidic leader. Taught, and illustrated, the importance of silence.

WERFEL, FRANZ. (1890-1945) Born in Prague. Austrian novelist, playwright and poet. Influenced by many spiritual and intellectual movements including mystic Catholicism. With the rise of Fascism returned to Judaism. Wrote *"The Song of Bermadette", "Hearken unto the Voice"*, etc. Settled in America 1940, in Beverley Hills, California.

WOLF, ZEV, OF ZBARAZH. (d. 1800) Third generation Chasidic leader, renowned for his kindness and humility.

WOLFSKEHL, KARL. (1868-1948) Born Darmstadt, died in New Zealand. Leader of Stefan George school of poetry in pre-Nazi times, turned more and more to Jewish identity with rise of antisemitism. Wrote a book-length poem called *"1933"*.

WOUK, HERMAN. (1915-) American novelist and playwright. Orthodox Jew, author of *"This Is My God"*.

YEHOASH. (SOLOMON BLOOMGARTEN). (1870-1927) Yiddish poet. Born in Russia, emigrated to America in 1890. Translated the Bible into Yiddish.

YERUSHALMI. (See *Talmud).

YETZER. Inclination, impulse, urge or drive. Term in rabbinic psychology for the two drives in man: towards good (Yetzer Tov) and towards evil (Yetzer HaRa). The "evil impulse" is not evil per se, but is the "passion" in which all human action originates, which may be channelled towards the good and holy.

GLOSSARY

YITZHAK MEIR ROTHENBERG ALTER OF GER (GUR). (1789-1866) Founder of the Ger chasidic dynasty. Talmudic scholar, fought to preserve tradition against changes imposed by the government. Involved himself with the problems of the masses, trying to win them over to Torah study.

YOMA (The Day). Fifth tractate of the *Mishnah, order *Moed* (seasons). Deals with the Day of Atonement.

ZADDIK. The leader of the chasidic community.

ZALMAN, SHNEOR OF LIADY. (THE RAV). (1746-1813) Founder of system of *"Chabad"* Chasidism. (CHaBaD is derived from *CHochmah, Binah, Da'at* – wisdom, reason, knowledge.) Emphasised intellectual rationalism, traditional rabbinic study and mysticism within the chasidic movement.

ZOHAR (Brightness). Main work of Spanish Kabbalah in four parts, mainly as a commentary on the Pentateuch and Song of Songs, Ruth and Lamentations. Probably two authors. End of the 13th Century.

ZUSYA OF HANIPOL. (d. 1800) Early Chasidic leader, one of the best known heroes of chasidic folktales – about his wanderings as a young man with his brother *Elimelech of Lizensk. A simple, modest and kind man, an example of innocence and personal righteousness.

ZWEIG, STEFAN. (1881-1942) Austrian biographer, essayist, playwright and poet. As a refugee from the Nazis, he died in Rio de Janeiro in a suicide pact with his wife.

ACKNOWLEDGMENTS

The editor acknowledges his indebtedness to the members of the RSGB Prayer Book Committee under the chairmanship of Rabbi Hugo Gryn, for their guidance in the preparation of this anthology, and all his colleagues on the Assembly of Ministers for helpful comments and suggestions.

My particular thanks go to Rabbi Lionel Blue for help in the initial editing, and to Mrs. Joy Goldman for her invaluable patience and care in preparing the manuscripts.

The publishers are indebted to the following for their kind permission to reproduce copyright material in this book:

George Allen & Unwin Ltd. for an extract from *God and Man in the Old Testament* by Leon Roth; Mr. N. Ausubel for an extract from *The Treasury of Jewish Poetry;* Behrman House Inc. for extracts from *Jewish Ethics, Philosophy and Mysticism* by Rabbi Louis Jacobs; Dr. E. Berkovits for an extract from an article which first appeared in *Tradition,* Vol. 8, No. 2; and for extracts from articles which first appeared in *Judaism,* Fall 1959 and Winter 1973; B'nai B'rith for extracts from *Great Jewish Ideas* edited by Abraham Ezra Millgram; The Bodley Head for an extract from *A Link in the Chain* by Eugene Heimler; Rabbi W. G. Braude for an extract from his sermon *What I learned in Alabama about Yarmulkes;* Calder and Boyars Ltd. for extracts from *Prison Poems* by Yuli Daniel, translated by D. Burg and A. Boyars;; Doubleday & Co. Inc. for excerpts from *This is My God* by Herman Wouk, © 1959, 1970 by The Abe Wouk Foundation, Inc.; Cassell & Co. Ltd. for an extract from *The World of Yesterday* by Stefan Zweig; City Lights for an extract from *Kaddish & Other Poems* by Allen Ginsberg; James Clarke & Co. Ltd. for an extract from *The Jewish Home* by Rabbi I. Maybaum; Collins Publishers for extracts from *Between Man and Man* by Martin Buber; Darton Longman & Todd Ltd. for an extract from *A Jewish Theology* by Rabbi Louis Jacobs, and from *To Heaven with Scribes and Pharisees* by Rabbi Lionel Blue; from *Everyman's Talmud* by Dr. A. Cohen, an Everyman's Library edition. Published in the United States by E. P. Dutton and reprinted with their permission; European Judaism for extracts from: *A Son of Man* by Natalia Ginzburg, translated by Richard Burns; *The Daemonic in Religion* by Werner Pelz; a collection of poems entitled *Quatrains* by Jacob Israel de Haan, translated by David Soetendorp; and *Where* by Arthur Jacobs; Farrar, Straus & Giroux, Inc. for extracts from *Man Is Not Alone* by Abraham J. Heschel © 1966, *O The Chimneys* by Nelly Sachs, translated by Michael Hamburger © 1967; Philipp Feldheim, Inc. for extracts from *Gates of Repentance,* translated by Shraga Silverstein; Gregg International Publishers Ltd. for an extract from *The Old Rabbinic Doctrine of God* by A. Marmorstein, 1969; Victor Gollancz Ltd. for an extract from *God Is No More* by Werner and Lotte Pelz, and from *My Dear Timothy* by V. Gollancz; Harcourt Brace Jovanovich, Inc. for an extract from *Heinrich Heine: Paradox and Poet,* translated by Louis I. Untermeyer; Hebrew Publishing Company, New York, for extracts from *Code of Jewish Law* by Rabbi Solomon Ganzfried, translated by Hyman E. Goldin 1927; Mr. Samuel Hertz for extracts from *The Authorized Daily Prayer Book* with commentary by the late Dr. J. H. Hertz, and from *A Book of Jewish Thoughts* selected and arranged by the late Dr. J. H. Hertz; David Higham Associates Ltd. for an extract from *The Jewish Poets of Spain,* translated by David Goldstein; Hodder and Stoughton Ltd. for an extract from *Man's Search for Meaning* by Viktor Frankl; Hutchinson Publishing Group Ltd. for an extract from *Between Heaven and Earth* by Franz Werfel; The Jewish Agency for Israel for an extract from *The Quality of Faith* by S. H. Bergman; Jewish Chronicle Publications for extracts from *A Guide to Yom Kippur* and from *A Guide to Rosh Ha-Shanah* by Rabbi Louis Jacobs; The Jewish Publication Society of America for extracts from the following:

ACKNOWLEDGMENTS

The Yom Kippur Anthology and *The Rosh Hashanah Anthology* by Philip Goodman; *Selected Religious Poems of Solomon Ibn Gabirol* translated by Israel Zangwill; *Selected Poems of Jehudah Halevi* translated by Nina Salaman; *Post-Biblical Hebrew Literature* by B. Halper; *Jewish Life in the Middle Ages* by Israel Abrahams; Mr. J. Sonntag for an extract from an article by J. L. Talmon in *Jewish Writing Today*, Vol. 21, 1973; the executors of the late Rev. Morris Joseph for an extract from *Judaism as Creed and Life*, published by Routledge and Kegan Paul Ltd; Ktav Publishing House, Inc. for extracts from *Understanding Jewish Prayer* by Rabbi J. Petuchowski; Granada Publishing Ltd. for an extract from *Modern Russian Poetry* by Vladimir Markev and Merrill Sparks; Macmillan, London and Basingstoke for extracts from *A Rabbinic Anthology* by Montefiore and Loewe, and from *Truth in Religion and Other Sermons* by C. G. Montefiore, 1906; The National Book League for an extract by Moses Ibn Ezra, translated by A. C. Jacobs, from *Books*, Autumn 1974; New York University Press for an extract from *Heine: The Artist in Revolt* by Max Brod, ©1962 by New York University; Routledge & Kegan Paul Ltd. for extracts from *The Jewish Year: With Other Devotional Poems* by Alice Lucas; Russell & Volkening, Inc. for extracts from *Basic Judaism* by Rabbi Milton Steinberg; Hilda Schiff for a poem published in *Transatlantic Review*, Autumn 1966; Schocken Books Inc. for extracts from the following: *The Hasidic Anthology* by Louis I. Newman,©1934 by Charles Scribner's Sons, ©1963 Schocken Books Inc; *Ten Rungs: Hasidic Sayings* by Martin Buber ©1947; *The Penal Colony* by Franz Kafka,©1948, copyright renewed ©1975 by Schoken Books Inc. , *Aspects of Rabbinic Theology* by Solomon Schechter; *The Essence of Judaism* by Leo Baeck ©1948; Professor S. Schwarzschild for extracts from an article entitled Speech and Silence before God, which first appeared in *Judaism*, Summer 1961; The Publications Committee of the United Synagogue for extracts from *Penitence, Prayer and Charity* by Rabbi Raymond Apple; Vallentine, Mitchell & Co. Ltd. for an extract from *The Diary of Anne Frank*, 1952, and from *The Path of Life* by the Rev. V. G. Simmons, 1961; The Viking Press, Inc. for extracts from *The Good Society* edited by Norman Lamm, ©1974 B'nai B'rith Commission on Adult Jewish Education; Vincent & Stuart Publishers Ltd. (Robinson & Watkins Books Ltd.) for extracts from *The Way of Man: According to the Teaching of Hasidism* by Martin Buber; The European Board of the World Union for Progressive Judaism for extracts from *In Memoriam Leo Baeck;* The World Union for Progressive Judaism for extracts from *The Growth of Reform Judaism* by W. Gunther Plaut; Thomas Yoseloff Ltd. and A. S. Barnes & Co. Inc. for extracts from *A Treasury of Jewish Quotations* edited by J. L. Baron; *The Way We Think* by J. Leftwich; and *The Golden Peacock: an Anthology of Yiddish Poetry* edited by J. Leftwich; Rabbi I. Maybaum, Rabbi J. Newman, Rabbi S. Sperber and Rabbi A. Steinsalz for previously unpublished material. Bloch Publishing Co. Inc. for extracts from *Maggidim and Hasidim: Their Wisdom* edited by Louis I. Newman, and from *God and Man in the Sefer Hasidim* by Simon G. Kramer. Commentary for extracts first published in that magazine and subsequently *The Treasury of Jewish Poetry*, published by Crown Publishers Inc., and an extract from an article *Going to Shule* by Mr. Milton Himmelfarb, April 1966. Holt, Rinehart and Winston, Inc. for an extract from *Tonight* by Zishe Landau, translated by Edward Field from *A Treasury of Yiddish Poetry*, edited by Irving Howe and Eliezer Greenberg.Copyright © 1969 by Irving Howe and Eliezer Greenberg.

Thames and Hudson Ltd. for an extract from *The Informed Heart* by Bruno Bettelheim; Mrs. Sylvia Heschel for an extract from an article *On Prayer* by A. J. Heschel in Conservative Judaism, Fall 1970; Rabbi A. Holtz for the translation of an extract from an article by Elisha Rodin in *Judaism*, Fall 1965; Thomas Y. Crowell Co. Inc. for an extract from *The Judaic Tradition* edited by Nahum N. Glatzer; Schocken Books Inc. for extracts from the following: *Tales of the Hasidim: The Early Masters* by Martin Buber, ©1947; *On Judaism* by Martin Buber, ©1967; *Israel and the World* by Martin Buber, ©1948, 1963; *Franz Rosenzweig: His Life and Thought* presented by Nahum N. Glatzer, ©1953, 1961; *Days of Awe* by S. Y. Agnon, ©1948, 1956; Ernst Simon's "Law and Observance in Jewish Experience" in *Tradition and Contemporary Experience* edited by Alfred Jospe, ©1970 by B'nai B'rith Hillel Foundations, Inc; *1933 A Poem Sequence* by Karl Wolfskehl,©1947

Whilst every effort has been made to trace copyright owners of the material used, the publishers take this opportunity of tendering apologies to any owners whose rights may have been unwittingly infringed.